A ticket-of-leave man

Convict Life

Or, Revelations Concerning Convicts and Convict Prisons

A ticket-of-leave man

Convict Life
Or, Revelations Concerning Convicts and Convict Prisons

ISBN/EAN: 9783744784269

Printed in Europe, USA, Canada, Australia, Japan

Cover: Foto ©ninafisch / pixelio.de

More available books at **www.hansebooks.com**

CONVICT LIFE;

OR,

REVELATIONS CONCERNING CONVICTS AND CONVICT PRISONS.

BY

A TICKET-OF-LEAVE MAN.

LONDON:
WYMAN & SONS, 81, GREAT QUEEN STREET,
LINCOLN'S-INN FIELDS, W.C.
1879.
All Rights Reserved.

WYMAN AND SONS, PRINTERS,
GREAT QUEEN STREET, LINCOLN'S INN FIELDS,
LONDON, W.C.

PREFACE.

IT is hoped that these pages may be read with interest, not only as a truthful record of Convict Life, but also as a contribution towards Convict-Prison Reform. The writer has at least one qualification entitling him to express an opinion on this important subject: he writes — alas! — from personal experience. Many names which would have added confirmation to the facts recited, have for obvious reasons been omitted.

LONDON, 30*th September*, 1879.

CONTENTS.

Chapter	Page
I.—Introductory	1
II.—Crime and Criminals	8
III.—Convict Labour and Convict Association	33
IV.—Prison Life—Convicts and their Guardians	71
V.—Convicts and their Guardians (*continued*)	90
VI.—Convicts and their Guardians: Prison Punishments, &c.	116
VII.—Reformatory and Sanatory	160
VIII.—Report of the Commission	199
IX.—Suggestions and Summary	238
Postscript	249

CONVICT LIFE.

CHAPTER I.

INTRODUCTORY.

IN the following pages I intend to expose some of the evils connected with the English convict system, and in the interests of society to suggest some remedies. I must be very candid at the outset and confess that all the knowledge I possess on this subject has been gained by a sad and bitter experience. After living up to middle life in the character of a gentleman, and with the reputation of an honourable man, I was weak enough to allow a terrible domestic affliction to drive me into dissipation, and the end of my madness was the committal of an act for which the law claimed me as its victim. An English judge, who has since gone to that bourn from which not even judges return, thought it to be his duty, for the sake of example, to send a man of some respectability and education, and who had never before darkened the doors of a police-court, to herd with professional thieves in penal servitude for seven years.

I will not say that I did not deserve this sentence, for I look back upon my own misconduct with feelings of shame, horror, and disgust; but I feel bound to say, in the interests of society and the taxpayer, that six months of solitary confinement, with assiduous labour, rough food, and a hard bed, would have been quite as efficacious, and would not have exposed me to the evil influences and vile associations which have surrounded me during the past six years, and which it has required no small amount of moral courage on my part to withstand. Not very long ago I was released upon licence, or what is generally known as a "ticket of leave." I have stated these facts that my readers may be assured that I know something of the subject upon which I am writing. I know that I have degraded myself, work by doing one themselves, and that they never will;" but the *proceeds* of that labour, or any other property which they can appropriate, either by sneaking trickery or brutal violence, they look upon as fair game; and, by some mysterious delusion which seems to obfuscate their mental and moral senses, I almost believe that they are sincere in regarding the law which punishes them as a persecutor and a tyrant. In speaking of themselves they invariably try to identify themselves with the *working* classes, ignoring altogether the self-evident fact, that the security afforded by the law to property is more important and necessary to the working man than to the millionaire.

I think it was Jeremy Bentham who said, that the law does not profess to give men property, but it gives them a *security* for the safe-keeping of their honestly-acquired possessions. Without the law there would be no security for the acquirements of the enterprising merchant, for *the furniture of the poor man's cottage,* or for *the results of a week of honest toil.* Bentham's own words just occur to me: " Without law there is no security ; consequently no abundance, nor even certain subsistence. And the only equality which can exist in such a condition is the equality of misery."

I think that miscreants who prefer thieving to work, and whose consciences are so elastic that they "make no bones" about systematically appropriating the results of the industry of honest men, should not be pampered. I think they should be made to feel, and to feel acutely, that "the way of the transgressor is hard." I have nothing in common with those who try to create any sympathy for thieves on account of the hideous dress they have to wear, or because their hair is cropped, or their beds hard, or their beef tough. I have lived among these thieves for six years, and for the future I shall close my ears to all such claptrap complaints. A man who lives for no other purpose and with no other object than to break the laws of his country has no right to expect "kid-glove treatment," and I do not think should be allowed to revel in the luxuries which may be obtained at "Blanchard's" or the "Star and Garter."

In the outside world the great object of his life has been to live without work, and to obtain dishonestly the means of pampering his appetite. The professional thief has no higher aspiration than to gratify his animal nature, and if he could do this in prison, incarceration would be no punishment to him. The law acts wisely in depriving thieves of alcohol and tobacco, and in giving them only so much as is necessary of coarse and wholesome food; but it ought to go further than this, and compel all prisoners to earn their subsistence, unless they are physically incapacitated for so doing. They should be taught the value and the importance of work, and be allowed by their own industry to provide a fund with which to begin the world afresh when they are released. I am very well aware that there is a very large class of professional criminals upon which no system can hope to work any reform; and that brings me to the great and crying evil of the existing organization,—the indiscriminate association of prisoners. At present the English convict prisons are breeding-dens for the procreation of professional thieves. A boy who has committed a drunken assault is placed under the tuition of the hero of a hundred burglaries. "Hodge," who during his previous life has been—in a Carlylean sense—a religious man, and has existed upon the proceeds of "divine labour," goes to Portland, and is there initiated into the mysteries of an art which, upon his release, will enable him to live upon the labour of others.

A London clerk (perhaps an underpaid one and with a large family) has forgotten for a moment that "honesty is the best policy." His associations up to the time of his "lapse" had been moral and virtuous. In a weak moment he takes a stray sovereign from the petty-cash drawer. He is sent to Dartmoor, and upon his release—thanks to the good fellowship of the men amongst whom the Government places him for punishment and reform—he is able to open a cash-box, and close it again, without the use of a key. I propose in the following pages to expose these evils and to suggest some remedies for them.

CHAPTER II.

CRIME AND CRIMINALS.

IT may be interesting to take a rapid glance at the various classes of criminals with which the law has to deal. In the front rank there is a class, happily few in number, who become thieves from a sheer lack of conscience; men who do not act under the influence of liquor, and who are not prompted by the goadings of poverty, but who, seeing that they can with ease, or by the use of a little chicanery, possess themselves of the property of others, allow no feelings of honour or justice to stand in their way. I have no doubt that envy is one of the most powerful incentives to crime with this class. Fortunate circumstance, or accident, has thrown them into the society of men whose means are greater than their own; they immediately imbibe a desire to rival their associates in luxury and display, and, having no moral principles to restrain them, do not hesitate to take a short but crooked cut to wealth.

There have been many examples of this class in very recent times. Amongst the most notable are Redpath, Paul, William Roupell, and the four Yankees who in 1873 made so formidable a raid upon the Bank of England. I must admit, that I can draw no moral distinction between these men and the midnight burglar. Catherine Webster certainly adopted a more coarse and brutal method of obtaining what did not belong to her; but, if weighed against one of the distinguished criminals I have named, the circumstances and advantages of each being taken into account, I am inclined to think that the balance would be in the woman's favour. The man who deliberately and in cold blood, and with no excuse of poverty or temporary distress to urge him, but merely for the sake of personal aggrandisement, and to gratify his pride and love of luxury and display, systematically plots to rob and defraud others, forfeits, I think, all claim to mercy on account of his social position, and may be safely and justly consigned to the same description of punishment as awaits the highway robber.

Lower down in the social scale, but standing morally upon the same platform, is that great class which seems to increase every year in the same ratio as the population. Stealing is to a very great extent hereditary in England. There are thousands of thieves to-day whose fathers and mothers were as familiar with the interior of half the prisons of England as they are. Many of them were born in prison; many more in the workhouse; and nearly all of them, have, from their very cradle, lived in an atmosphere of vice. Whether the law has fulfilled its duty to society in allowing well-known and habitual criminals to have charge of their offspring, and to train them as lawbreakers, is a question I cannot now entertain; but we all know that it does allow it, and makes no attempt to interfere, until it is called upon to punish. A clever professional thief whom I met at Portland two years ago, and who hailed from Birmingham, told me that he got his first lessons in filching from his mother. His father, he told me, was an "honest working man," and was porter in a grocery establishment. This father was always "square," never committing himself, or falling into the hands of the police. His mother had made a pair of drawers which were double, and formed a sort of bag; into these drawers the father used to drop any stray tea or coffee with which he came in contact in the course of his duties, and which he thought would not be needed by his employer. When, as often happened, the quantity brought home was too large for the requirements of the family, it was disposed of to a neighbouring *publican* in exchange for a beverage which inspired this *honest working man* with courage to obtain fresh supplies. This thief asserted that there were publicans in a very poor neighbourhood to be *trusted*, and who were never so inquisitive as other people.

The idea of morality entertained by this class may be judged of from the fact that this prisoner used to boast that his father was a very "square" man; what he meant, of course, was that he had never been caught. The mother, who was his tutor, he admitted was crooked, and had been in prison more than once. When my informant was a child of five, he would be taken by this mother to a shoe-shop on a busy Saturday night. The woman would be difficult to fit, and whilst the shopman was employed in searching for the necessary size, the child, who sat upon the floor, was attaching to some hooks under his mother's dress two or three pairs of shoes. These acts of dexterity, which, of course, had been rehearsed at home, were rewarded by presents of candy and halfpence, and, in obedience to the inflexible law of cause and effect, the son, as he grew into manhood, became an accomplished professional thief. My prison experiences have taught me that this is no solitary case, but merely an example of every-day life. Many of this thief-class come into the custody of the police as mere children; but they either escape with some slight punishment, and return to their old haunts, or, if sent to a reformatory-school, they are thrown into close association with a few hundred other young thieves, who, like themselves, have been spawned upon the dunghills of our great cities; who have, like themselves, been left by the Law itself to grow up under the maternal wing of thieves; and who have sucked vice into their nature from degraded mothers, whose breasts have at the same time inoculated their physical system with poisoned gin.

With such an education as I have indicated, it is not very singular that the hereditary English thief should develop into a villain of the very deepest dye, which he certainly does.

My sincere conviction, after six years of life amongst them, is, that as a class, and with very few exceptions, they are utterly and irreclaimably lost. They are so vile, and so filthy, that no reformatory system under God's sun would have the slightest chance of inspiring their cursed natures with one pure thought or one honest aspiration. I had almost said, it would be a bright day for England if four or five thousand of the wretches now confined in convict prisons could be embarked in the *Great Eastern*, towed into mid-ocean, and sunk in its fathomless depths. I have no expectation that the British Government will adopt this summary method of disposing of them, and I shall, therefore, in another chapter suggest some more tangible scheme which will relieve society of this intolerable incubus. I hope also by-and-by to expose some of the tricks and dodges by which thieves defraud the public. In this place I must confine myself to a description of their moral characteristics. They are, in a word, dead to all sense of shame. They are cowardly brutes, and their animal instincts have crowded every human feeling out of their nature. They have all the same "leary" look, and an unmistakable cunning stares at you out of every feature. They have all been educated in Government schools; for after emerging from the reformatory, they have graduated under the ægis of those licensed-dens of infamy, the public-house and the gin-palace, from the profits of which England derives so large a portion of her revenue. I am not a professed teetotaler, but compulsory association with the brutes that have been created and reared under the immediate influence of whisky-shops, has forced me to the conclusion that to keep an establishment where liquors are sold over a bar to be drunk on the premises is about the meanest thing a man can do in this world to obtain a living. But to go back to the character of these professional thieves. They are entirely destitute of all manliness. They could no more stand up, self-supported, than the ivy could rear itself like the oak. They are equally destitute of natural and acquired strength. They approach most thoroughly to the idea of universal and consummate depravity. They think nothing of passing their lives in inflicting misery upon their fellow-creatures, and they do it not only with satisfaction, but with a hideous rapture. If they can commit robberies without violence, they only prefer to do so because they avoid all risk of the "cat," which is the only thing they fear, and which I think, therefore, should be liberally administered; but if the robbery cannot be effected quietly they do not scruple to use the knife or the bludgeon, buoying themselves up with the hope that they will escape detection, which three times out of four they do. Their social habits are as filthy inside the prison, as no doubt they are in the rookeries which they call their homes. They have a strange disposition to filthiness and dirt in all senses of the words, and the hog is a sweeter animal by far. They have also a *penchant* for horrible vices, which I regret to say they get opportunities to commit, even in what are called "separate prisons." I am certain that if the sensuality, the poltroonery, the baseness, the effrontery, the mendacity, and the barbarity which distinguish the every-day life of these professional thieves were depicted in the character of a hero in a criminal romance it would be set down as a caricature. I am not exaggerating : I solemnly declare that whatsoever things are unjust, whatsoever things are filthy, whatsoever things are hateful and fiendish, if there be any vice and infamy deeper and more horrible than all other vice and infamy, it may be found ingrained in the character of the English professional thief. Compared with him Gulliver's "Yahoos" were cultivated gentlemen.

Whenever these hopefuls are caught and drafted into a convict prison, they set their cunning to work to pass what they call an "easy lagging," and the truth is, that they get through their sentences with less than half the difficulty and less than half the punishment experienced by *green* hands such as I was. They become the tools of the turnkeys, themselves culled for the most part from the very dregs of the population. They—these adepts in crime—lend themselves as tools to the turnkeys in catching unawares the amateurs in any breakage of the prison rules; in fact, caged and no longer able to prey upon society out-of-doors, they descend to a vocation compared with which even the life of a pickpocket or a pimp is honourable. I have not quite done with them; I have to cap the climax. Add to this glorious assemblage of qualities, a high profession of contrition and piety whenever the prison chaplain approaches them; an anxious desire—of course to serve some cunning end—to partake as often as possible of the Sacrament of the "Lord's Supper," to be prominent members of the church choir; to be loud in their responses, and to attract the notice of governors and chaplains by the obtrusive reverence of their behaviour in church, and I think you have an effect which is overpowering.

I am anxious that my readers should keep the character of this class in their mind when they come to read what I have to say by-and-by about the indiscriminate association of prisoners, because it should be remembered that this is by far the most numerous of the different classes of prisoners which the law has to take care of; and having described their characters, I need hardly add that in every prison they are the ruling power, the reigning influence, the active spirit.

Then the law has to deal with another class of criminals for whom I would ask neither consideration nor mercy, miscreants who seem dead to the commonest and most natural instincts of humanity,—men and women who are guilty of the most hideous and barbarous crimes, acts of violence and brutality which are truly appalling in their nature. Some of my readers will recollect the circumstance of the "Penge murder" not quite two years ago; a case in which two men and two women conspired to starve to death a half-witted relative, and who actually made themselves merry within the sound of her dying cries.

One of these wretches, Patrick Staunton, was a fellow-prisoner of mine at Dartmoor, and I saw him not long ago *snivelling* and *crying* because he had to eat his bread without butter, and because he was made to perform a little—and a very little—light labour. I ask no consideration or mercy for monsters of this sort, the law certainly does not deal too hardly with them. This Patrick Staunton is always running after the prison doctor, and begging for medicine and relief from work. The medicine I would have administered to reptiles of the Patrick Staunton class would be "three dozen" at the triangle when the sun dawns upon the first of every month.

But now let me turn to classes for whom I would claim some consideration, and who ought not to be considered as habitual criminals or be dealt with as such. There is, first of all, the man of education and culture, who, perhaps in the presence of some great calamity, or from misfortunes in his business, or to ward off poverty from those nearest and dearest to him, in some rash moment, and after a life of sterling honesty and integrity, commits one act of dishonesty. I am reminded of cases now, where, if a little time had been given and a little consideration extended, men with honest hearts, who are now in penal servitude, might have refunded money which they were induced to take, and have been living in happiness and respectability with their families. I know one man now at Portland under a long sentence, who was the post-master of a northern town. He was one of the most guileless men I ever knew. I thoroughly believe that he would rather die than defraud a man of a penny. He had a brother who was dear to him, but not in so good a position as himself. The brother came from a distant town one morning, wanting a hundred pounds in a hurry to save his home from destruction and his furniture from the auctioneer's hammer. The post-master had investments which he could not immediately realize. He did not expect a visit from the Post-office Surveyor for ten days. He borrowed the Post-office money to save his brother. Without doubt, if things had taken their usual course, he would have replaced the money.

Unfortunately for him the Surveyor—perhaps receiving a hint from the proverbial "good-natured friend" who wanted the post-mastership—turned up the next day, the money was not forthcoming, and the poor post-master got either ten or twelve years, I forget which.

I know another prisoner at Portland under a long sentence; I believe him to be one of the purest-minded and most honest-hearted men in the world. His character up to the time of the act for which he was convicted had been, perhaps, as spotless as that of the best of the human family. His brother is a partner in an old-established firm of high respectability in Piccadilly. His son has, during his father's incarceration, passed through one examination after another in his chosen profession with distinguished honour. I shall not easily forget the emotion of my poor prison friend, when reading the letters which conveyed to him the news of his dear son's success, and which told how good God had been to his loved wife and daughters in his absence. I cannot help believing that A—— was a good father and a good man. He was in a position of trust; one day in an evil moment for him, and in his anxiety to shield the family of an old friend from disaster, he took money which did not belong to him. He took it for an act of charity; he took it knowing that he could repay it; *but*, in doing so, he no doubt acted dishonestly, and he had to pay the penalty.

I know of many similar cases, but I will not detail them now. I do not wish to be misunderstood. I make no apology for the acts of these men. They make none for themselves. They are convinced, as I am, that it is the duty of the law to punish in such cases. Unless it were to do so there would be no security for property of any sort. But there are *degrees* of guilt; and I venture to suggest that this class of men are not abandoned and hardened and hopeless criminals, and should not be dealt with as such. I am quite sure that six months of imprisonment would be to such men a much more severe punishment than the seven years of penal servitude to an old thief. To a man of education and respectability, who has for once yielded to temptation—and surely to err is human—the very first result of his act is almost a sufficient punishment. He commits a moral suicide; he entails upon himself ruin and disgrace, often the loss of friendship on the part even of his relatives; he is torn from all that makes life dear to him; to say nothing of the hell of remorse with which a man of any culture and refinement is haunted in the seclusion of his prison cell when he contemplates his own downfal.

I repeat, that I make no apology for the acts of this class of prisoners; but they are not brutes, they are not monsters, they are far different to habitual criminals, or professional thieves. They are erring men, in nearly every case deeply sensible of their guilt, and deeply penitent. This class of men *never* offends a second time; and I do not think it necessary in the interests of law and order that they should be treated as, or herded with, professional thieves and red-handed murderers.

It should be remembered too, that amongst those who are convicted for the first time, the law often has within its clutches men who are innocent. The case of Habron is too fresh in the memory of the public to need remark here; but his was not a solitary case.

A few weeks ago, Mr. Cross, acting in the interests of justice, found it desirable to release another man, who for four years had been separated from a newly-married and sorrowful young wife, and condemned to the society of the infamous at Portland.

Thomas Scampton, a young manufacturer, whose family have for generations pursued their avocations with honour in the town of Leicester, was charged with making a bonfire of his own factory to secure in ready money the sum for which it was insured.

The chief witness against him was his own partner, with whom he had been at variance. There was hard swearing, and there were interested motives on the side of the prosecution. The jury convicted, but afterwards petitioned for the prisoner's release. At last, finding that Mr. Cross and Baron Bramwell were deaf to all appeals, the family, conscious of their loved one's innocence, indicted the man who was principal witness against him for perjury. At this trial, although the prosecution failed to convict, so much evidence transpired to prove Scampton's innocence, that upon the representation of Lord Justice Thesiger, he was immediately released. I worked side by side with this man on the "trawleys" at Portland. I was a witness of the anguish which he suffered, more on his young wife's account than his own. It was his custom to work by my side when he could, and we together tried to escape the contagion of the moral pestilence by which we were surrounded. Scampton called upon me a day or two ago. He says that he can hardly yet realize his deliverance from the association of "the awful denizens" of Portland, and that often in the society of his devoted and pure young wife, the hideous oaths of the gaol-birds still ring in his ears and cause him to shudder at the remembrance of the pollution which was forced upon him.

Another class for whom I would ask some consideration, are men who were born before the School Board was so active as it is now—very ignorant, knowing veritably no difference between

B and a bull's foot, and who are also very, very poor. Men naturally honest, and desiring to remain so, who, during as severe a winter as that of 1878-79, find themselves utterly unable, no matter how much they may try, to obtain employment, have, in the extremity of their need, carried off from some neighbouring farmer's barn a bushel of potatoes, or from some adjacent baker's shop a gallon of bread, with which to satisfy the cravings of a dozen helpless and innocent children. It may be doubted by some whether such cases are ever punished by penal servitude; but the sentence is very commonly inflicted under these precise circumstances, and especially when the culprit happens to be tried by "the great unpaid" at Quarter Sessions. The man, perhaps acting under the delusion that God made rabbits for poor men when he made hares for the rich, has had a previous conviction for some poaching affray. Now I am not defending poaching, and I agree that whatever the law may be, the duty of a good citizen is to obey it; but as the law of bygone times allowed the last generation to grow up in stolid ignorance, I think some little allowance should be made for this class, and that a former conviction for poaching should not be deemed a sufficient reason for sending a man to penal servitude for a solitary instance of dishonesty, committed to save his family from starvation. Thefts of all sorts must be punished, but again I say, the men who commit such petty thefts are not monsters, or murderers, or professional thieves, and should not be herded with them.

I will take this opportunity to make public an order which has been given by his Royal Highness the Prince of Wales to the servants and keepers on his estate in Norfolk. The Prince of Wales gets a good deal of abuse, undeserved abuse, from all sorts of people; but what I have to tell about him speaks volumes for his goodness of heart, and if his example were followed by all the landowners in the country, a large number of crimes would be prevented. A prisoner now undergoing sentence for a poaching affray upon another estate in Norfolk, told me that he formerly lived in the neighbourhood of Sandringham. I will use his own words. He said, "I was never in trouble while I lived *there, nor nobody else.*" I asked him, why? He said, because if a man needed a dinner, and wanted a rabbit, he had only to go to the house and ask for one. The Prince had given special orders that the men about were *not* to trespass and shoot for themselves, but that his keepers were always to supply a rabbit to any labourer on the estate, and that if none were in hand they were immediately to go out and shoot some.

There is still another class of criminals who, I think, should not be herded with professional thieves, and whom a good reformatory system might transform into sober and honest citizens. I regret to say they include a very large class,— many men, many women, and, worse still, lots of boys and girls between the ages of fourteen and twenty, who commit crimes under the immediate influence of intoxicating drinks. Of course, I know what abject fools men and women are to get drunk, and that intoxication is a lame excuse for crime; but then the law allows so many inducements to be held out to people to get drunk that I really think it should be considered responsible in some degree for the result. There are many hundreds of prisoners now in convict prisons whose crimes were committed while they were in a state of drunkenness,—often in the public-house itself, always soon after emerging from it. Drink is such a common evil amongst the working-classes of Britain that it is rightly called the National Sin; and I think that the Government has so much encouraged the vice that it should not deal too hardly with its victims when they are honest men, but should anxiously educate them, when they become prisoners, into more excellent habits. There are numbers of lads now in our convict prisons who have committed criminal and other assaults when in a state of drunkenness who have never been guilty of dishonesty, but who are yet herded with professional thieves, and are not receiving any instruction or advice which may guard them from evil in the future.

The case of two youths, mere boys, just recurs to my memory. They are now at Portland under sentence of penal servitude for life. Their names are Drinkwater and Stonestreet, and they were sentenced to be hanged, but had their sentence commuted. They got drunk on a Saturday night, after a week of honest industry. At the public-house, and when in a maudlin state, they encountered a woman old enough to have been their mother; they treated her, and she got drunk. At midnight the landlord, who had supplied all the liquor, turned them into the street; the woman's head struck the curb, but she got up and went away with the lads. At daybreak on the Sunday morning the lads were found in a drunken sleep; the woman, who lay between them, and who had evidently been pulled about, was *dead*. I have inquired about these boys since my release. The affair took place at Southall, in Middlesex. The boys were honest and industrious, and my experience of them at Portland leads me to say that they were unusually artless and free from vice. When they first came to Portland they never used foul language, or took part in disgusting conversations, but I cannot hope that they will have any good qualities long if they remain in their present position amongst the professional thieves; and twenty years of such association will transform them into monsters.

I suppose that liquor, and the publican, and these boys caused the death of that woman; but I am quite satisfied that the boys know no more how she came to her death than I do. This is only one case of hundreds, nay, of thousands. I suppose that all the professional criminals of England were made so *originally*, either in their own persons or that of their progenitors, by *drink*, for if apparently by indolence or poverty, in nine cases out of ten the indolence and poverty were created by drink. I am quite certain that amongst *non*-professional criminals *nine-tenths* of their offences are *directly* traceable to *drink* and *public-houses*. It would be well for the working-classes of England if Dante's inscription were suspended over every gin-palace in the land:—

> Through me ye enter the abodes of woe;
> Through me to endless ruin ye are brought;
> Through me amongst the souls accurst ye go:
> All hope abandon, ye who enter here.

What is more to my purpose, though, is to

state my conviction that there is a large class of criminals who, though honest men, have broken the law while under the influence of drink; that although these men are justly punished, the law has another duty besides that of punishing them, and that is to *educate* and *reform them*. The duty of the law is not *only* to punish crime, but to use all the means in its power to prevent it for the future. It will be my aim in the following chapters to show, that there is a criminal responsibility attaching to the law for the manner in which it performs this duty; that under existing arrangements the law lays its hand the most heavily upon those who are the least guilty, because what to them is severe punishment is to the habitual gaol-bird no punishment at all; that the law owes it to the taxpayers, to society generally, and to a still higher power, to use all possible means to educate the ignorant, to raise the fallen, and to bring back the erring to a sense of their duty, but that at present its efforts in this direction are futile, and almost useless.

CHAPTER III.

CONVICT LABOUR AND CONVICT ASSOCIATION.

IT will be seen that in addition to a small number of educated professional criminals, and a large number of ignorant ones, the law has to deal with a variety of offenders who may be termed novices in crime. There are the educated, who have committed one wrong act; there is the large class who have committed all sorts of offences under the influence of liquor; there are the few unfortunates whom poverty has forced into crime; and there are numbers of mere children who ought never to have been sent into a convict prison at all. It may fairly be presumed that these classes are not intrinsically bad; that they are open to good influences; that a good reformatory system, judiciously worked, might transform them into industrious and sober and honest citizens.

Now, what does the present convict system do with these first offenders who do not yet belong to the class of habitual criminals? It sends them on to "public works," and thrusts them into close communion with the abandoned villains and professional thieves whose characteristics I described in the last chapter. It binds them as apprentices for five or seven years to learn the trade of law-breaking. They are, during the whole term of their imprisonment, under the influence, tuition, and example, of miscreants who, from the cradle to the grave, exist upon outrage and plunder; they are by these men initiated into all sorts of tricks and dodges by which they can evade the prison discipline, and elude the burden of work, *during* their imprisonment, and at the end of it enrol themselves in the great and yearly-increasing army of professional thieves.

They enter prison mere novices in crime: by the fostering care of a paternal Government in these "high schools" of rascality, they may upon their discharge be safely pronounced adepts in all the arts of thieving, and thoroughly qualified for a roguish career. An outsider will naturally ask how it is that opportunities are allowed for such free communication between prisoners, and I must reply by describing the system under which labour upon "public works" is carried on.

The men are organized into gangs or parties of about twenty-five each, under the supervision of a warder (or "screw" as he is called by prisoners). Every morning, weather permitting, the gangs are marched in double file to the scene of their labours, where they "break off" and commence the day's work. If it be stone-dressing, two men always work at one stone; if it is a "barrow-run," the "filler" and the wheeler are in close proximity; if it be trenching or brick-making, the men are almost of necessity close together, and they talk quietly, but incessantly, until the moment that the whistle blows to "fall-in" again.

So long as the men *appear* to be at work, no matter how little is done, and so long as they keep their eyes wide open in order to give "the office" to the warder as to the approach of a superior officer, they may talk as much as they please.

There is a tacit understanding between all "second-timers" and old thieves, and the officers who have charge of them. If the officer is caught in any dereliction of duty he is liable to a fine; these old thieves act as his spies, and take care that he is *not* caught. In return he allows the thieves to fetch what they call an easy lagging, to do as little work as they please, and to talk as much as they please — and *such* talk!

The language used by these old criminals is so abominable that I was going to say the Zulus or the Afghans would recoil from it with shame and horror; and the more revolting it is to decency the more it is enjoyed by the ignorant and degraded class of men who are selected by the authorities to superintend the labour, and assist in the *reformation* of convicts. In case of the approach of the governor or chief warder, and the possibility of their having heard what is going on, the officer in charge will make a report against a couple of men for talking or laughing at work. The men selected to be reported are invariably green hands, and the most innocent in the gang.

The reason for this is obvious: the old gaol-birds are content to act as spies for the warder, but, exercising the cunning which is one of the essentials of their vocation, they take pains to post themselves up in all his little weaknesses and derelictions of duty, and would not hesitate to betray him at some opportune moment, should he dare to report them. The small minority of warders who really do their duty, without fear or favour, have to be constantly on their guard, lest their heads should come in contact with bricks, or their bodies be found at the foot of a cliff.

Almost every officer in charge of a party has what are called his "marks," men who are made his scapegoats when he requires a sacrifice to propitiate his superiors and to sustain his own reputation for efficiency and discipline. These "marks" are in all cases the men who least deserve prison punishment. I have known an officer to get up a fictitious character for vigilance, and even to earn his promotion, by continually reporting two or three men of his party. The constitutions of these men were irretrievably ruined by the constant infliction of bread-and-water punishment, and yet I could swear that they were the least vicious and the most industrious in the gang.

But as I have heard these warders say, "We must look after them that look after us." The old thieves and they are old friends; they thoroughly understand each other, and work into each other's hands. The old thief fetches an "easy lagging," and recruits his health in anticipation of a new lease of criminal life; and the warder maintains his reputation for vigilance. The men who suffer, and who go to the wall, are the unsophisticated and the novices.

What wonder that with such associations, and under the influence of such a system, they lose all morality and manhood, and in sheer despair join the "regular army" of crime? In these conversations—and recollect, I am speaking from personal experience—the usual topic is the art of thieving; the causes of failure in daring burglaries; the mistakes by which, after a successful crime, the thieves failed to escape detection; the latest and newest invention for picking locks or opening safes; the most recent dodges for successful robberies at railway stations; the most eligible districts for shoplifting, and the most profitable occasions for pocket-picking. Notes are memorised by which former mistakes may be avoided, and the science of law-breaking made perfect. The novices are also instructed in the secrets and mysteries of the craft, the varied machinery existing in thieves' quarters for procuring alibis, false evidence, and other dodges for the evasion of the law.

They are regaled with exaggerated histories of successful schemes of plunder, and of the "glorious sprees" which have been enjoyed upon their fruits, and hundreds of the ignorant and the weak are by such tales induced to take their chance in the business as soon as they are liberated. I recollect one vagabond detailing his experiences at railway stations.

For twenty-five years he had successfully carried on a system of baggage-stealing; sometimes in clerical garb, sometimes as a swell-mobsman, and now and then disguised as an opulent agriculturist, he would manage to possess himself of valuable portmanteaus. Rugby, Derby, and Crewe were his favourite stations, but he had made several successful hauls from Charing-cross, by covering Dover labels with Croydon ones. Arrived at the latter station, the baggage was of course put out of the train, claimed by him, and disposed of in London before the real owners had arrived in Dover to miss it.

What surprised me most about this scoundrel was that his tongue did not betray him to the railway officials, for there could have been nothing about him except his clothes likely to deceive; a more veritable cad I never met. I forget how many hundreds of portmanteaus this man had possessed himself of, but for more than twenty years he lived luxuriously; the only intermissions being two short terms of imprisonment, and his present sentence of seven years' penal servitude.

He is now at Dartmoor, fetching what he calls

a very "easy lagging." He is considered by the warders a very "wide man"—a "man of the world." He looks after their interests, and they look after his. He is in the leather-cutting shop, and his labour is mere amusement. He is such a "wide man" that he never gets a report, and will consequently obtain the whole of his remission—nineteen months—and be discharged early next year upon a ticket-of-leave. He has a pupil in the same shop whom he is instructing in the mysteries of his art, and who is to become his assistant and accomplice in the future. The instructions go on in the presence of the officer in charge, who seems to enjoy the fun. The approach of the governor or chief warder may be seen from the windows of the shop; one prisoner is therefore always on the *qui vive* to give the alarm. The foul and disgusting conversation is incessant, but if "the authorities" enter all seems as quiet as the grave, and the warder looks as stern as a judge.

There is an old burglar and highway robber in the same shop who is now doing his third or fourth "lagging." From his experiences I might, had I been so inclined, have learned how to become a successful marauder. He has never done a day's work in his life, and never intends to; his great and constant regret is that he did not kill the poor old man upon whom, in the dead of night, and in a lonely house, he committed his last robbery; had he thoroughly "settled him," he says, there would have been no evidence to convict him. This old rascal, sixty years old, but hale and hearty, will get his discharge next Christmas, and has got all his arrangements made for a burglary at the house of a gentleman near Cambridge, acting upon information received from a prisoner recently arrived at Dartmoor, who was convicted on some other charge before he could effect the robbery himself. I cannot tell how many crimes are arranged in prison, and afterwards successfully carried out, but their name is Legion.

One scamp in the shoemaker's shop at Dartmoor, hearing that I was shortly to be discharged, and supposing me to be one of the "guild," requested me to carry a "crooked message" to his brother, whose address he gave me, and who, he said, was a "respectable working man." This brother, it seems, works at different houses as a mechanic, keeping *himself* straight, but informing his dishonest pals where there is a "good lay," and even taking impressions of keys which come into his possession in the course of his work, and by which ingress may be obtained at night to eligible premises.

The tenor of the message I was requested to convey was where some keys could be found which the prisoner had made to effect an entrance to a house in Great Portland-street, and a desire that the keys and necessary information might be handed over to another "pal."

More dangerous still are the conspiracies got up in prison between educated professional thieves. When at Portland I happened to be working near a celebrated convict, of diamond and chloroform renown. He, according to his own account, had lived luxuriously for years upon the proceeds of numberless ingenious schemes of dishonesty. His pal had been the successful floater of bubble companies, had once organized and paid for a grand testimonial and banquet to himself in the city of Dublin, the advertised reports of which in the *Times* and *Telegraph* induced lots of fools to invest in the bogus concern.

These two worthies were busily occupied during the year I was near them in bringing to perfection a scheme which threatened ruin to foreign bankers, principally upon the American continent. Both the rogues are now at liberty —one, as I am informed, being in New York, the other in London; and they are doubtless putting into operation the nice little game which they were allowed opportunities to concoct upon "public works."

I shall have to refer to these men again, but I give these details here, to show how faulty the present convict system is in regard to the association of prisoners, and still more for the purpose of urging the importance of a "classification of prisoners," so that first offenders and novices in crime may not be placed under the tuition of old thieves, and so be educated under the ægis of the law for a dishonest career.

I have just spoken of a man in the shoemaker's shop at Dartmoor. Shoemaking, of course, is indoor labour. In all the convict prisons the tailoring and shoemaking are pursued in large association rooms. Only a few weeks ago a murderous outrage was committed upon an officer in the shoemaker's shop at Dartmoor, an outrage which would have been impossible except where prisoners are associated.

The victim in this case, Luscombe, an assistant warder, is, if he be still alive, a shoemaker by trade, a native of Ashburton, Devonshire, and one of the few intelligent and respectable officers employed at Dartmoor. I saw him constantly while I was at that prison, and believe that, without fear or favour, and I am sure without any harshness, he tried to do his duty.

But he was one of the very few who was not "hail-fellow-well-met" with the old thieves; he had no sympathy with the "professional," and I always felt sure that he would at some time be made a victim for his want of policy.

If a novice in crime was put into the shop, a man who really desired to learn the trade with the view of turning it to good account afterwards, that man always found a friend in Luscombe.

But, of course, such men were industrious, for, as Luscombe often told them, "their object should be to see in how short a time they could make a good shoe." The few men in the shop who did this were called "Luscombe's lambs," "Government men," and "policemen," and were treated with contempt and derision by the old thieves. Why this is so, is evident. The policy of the professional thief is to do as little work as possible, to live at the expense of the country, and to give nothing in return; they never average more than three shoes a week— about a day's work for an industrious shoe- maker—so that the man who made three *pairs* a week, was their enemy, and the occasion of calling the attention of an honest officer to their laziness. I have very little doubt that when the truth comes out, it will be seen that Luscombe had reported one of these old thieves for laziness, and that for so doing he was made the victim of a conspiracy. More than nineteen officers out of twenty make themselves safe by letting all "professional" members of the "guild" do as they like; and this they will do so long as the prisoners are associated in large numbers, and have opportunities for conspiracy. It requires a man of great moral courage to do his duty under present regulations. Luscombe was one of these, but they are few and far between.

A description of this shoemaker's shop at Dartmoor, will convey a tolerable idea of the evils of the association of prisoners in all "public work" prisons; and the amount of labour performed in them will rather startle the innocents who suppose that one of the objects of the Convict Department is to transform criminals into industrious citizens.

In the early part of 1879 I myself *saw* sitting in this shop nearly two hundred men; more than one-half of them were *re*-convicted men; many had done two "laggings," some three, and a few four. Of the remaining half, about one-third had been in and out of prison all their lives for petty offences, but had managed to escape penal servitude. Sixty or seventy remain to be accounted for; these were first-offenders, many of them mere boys, convicted for drunken assaults, or for some poaching affray; youths and young men who, had they been sentenced to a short term of severe imprisonment, with coarse food and plenty of work, supplemented by the means of education, would very likely have turned out useful and honest citizens. Here they are, however, under the tutelage of old thieves, nominally to learn how to make a shoe, *really and truly* to be instructed in the most ingenious ways of filching a watch or a purse. The men are so crowded in this shop that they have to use very short threads for stitching their shoes, or their hands would come in contact with the next man's head; every facility, therefore, is afforded for chat.

It will no doubt appear strange to an outsider that so large a proportion of the criminal class should be shoemakers; the fact is that they are not; they have, however, in county prisons picked up a slight knowledge of cobbling, and of tailoring too, so that, when lagged, and asked their trade, they register themselves as shoemakers or tailors, knowing that in these trades they can "fetch" an "easy lagging," and have plenty of association with their pals. Not one in forty in this Dartmoor shop could make a shoe which would pass muster with the shoddiest manufacturer in Northampton; here, however, they are not only shoemakers but instructors too.

There are fifty old thieves sitting in different parts of the shop, each of whom has one or two youths—novices in crime as well as in shoemaking—under his instruction. What the apprentice learns during seven years of penal servitude may be easily guessed. I knew several who had been for three or four years under instruction who could just turn out—well, not a shoe, but what Carlyle would call an "amorphous botch," and they seemed to have no desire to improve so as to gain an honest livelihood in this branch of industry when discharged from prison, the reason being very obvious; they had learned from their teachers, not a "more excellent," but a much more easy method of obtaining money. I shall show presently that the law does nothing for the *regeneration* of criminals, but I think I *have* shown that it is very busily occupied in *creating* them. Sitting in such close proximity conversation is, of course, unlimited; and as all the professional thieves with whom I came in contact are dead to all sense of shame, the peculiar grossness of their immorality and obscenity comes out in their talk, and does its evil work in forming the character and habits of the new beginners in crime.

The bulk of the work performed in the shop consists of boots for the Metropolitan police force; the boots are supplied to the police at 9s. 3d. per pair, and as the material at contract price costs at least 8s. 3d., the prisoner who makes three boots in a week earns exactly 1s. 6d., or about the cost of the bread he eats, with no margin for the meat. This will be hard to believe, but as I was myself in the cutting-shop, where every piece of leather was shaped for the makers, I can speak very positively. In the middle of March last there were 190 shoemakers at work, and there were something less than 200 pairs of shoes manufactured in the week, so that, making every allowance for the hands employed upon the prison repairs, the work done did not average three shoes to the man in the week. If each man worked in his own cell he could, after three months' practice, make a pair of shoes every day with great ease, and would have no opportunity to corrupt others, or, if he be a novice, become himself corrupted. There would be no opportunity then for outrages such as that committed upon Luscombe. Learners should, of course, be instructed by competent officers and not by prisoners. There are four warders employed *nominally* at Dartmoor for this purpose—Roberts, Warren, Luscombe (the victim of the recent outrage), and a disagreeable fellow who rejoiced in the name of *Pinch*. The three first-named are doubtless competent men, but under the present regulations their duties are delegated to prisoners. If each man worked in his cell, two officers passing from one cell to another every few minutes might easily instruct all the learners, and with very advantageous results, not only to the prisoners but to the country.

The tailors' shops at Dartmoor, Portland, and the rest of the convict stations, are open to the same objections as to the association of prisoners. There are nearly a hundred tailors (?) at Dartmoor; far more than a hundred at Portland; from two to three hundred at Woking, and proportionate numbers in the other prisons. The only *tailoring* done is the clothing of the prison warders. The clothing of the prisoners is mere plain sewing, and, together with the repairs, might be easily performed by prisoners over sixty years of age, who are unfit for hard labour. The uniforms of the officers could be made by one-tenth part of the number now employed upon tailoring if the men worked in their cells, without the opportunity for "chat;" and I think that *this* work might well be confined to youths who are first offenders, and who really desire to learn a trade with a view to future honesty.

The present composition of the tailors' shops is this: Two-thirds able-bodied professional thieves, who have registered themselves as tailors to avoid hard labour, and the other third made up of old men, learners, and schemers, whose plausibility has imposed upon the doctors to excuse them from manual labour. Now, I very respectfully suggest that a thousand able-bodied but lazy men, who, when at large, religiously avoid all industrial pursuits, might with propriety be employed in some other way than in patching shirts and hatching schemes for the plunder of the public in the future. I do not think that the great army of professional thieves will be reduced, so long as its soldiers can, when in prison, enjoy the society of their chums, eat the bread of idleness, and sleep for ten hours out of the twenty-four in a comfortable hammock.

The men who do whatever hard work there is done on public works are, as I have said, novices and green hands, who have not been "wide" enough to register themselves as tailors or shoemakers.

The outdoor labour upon public works is as unprofitable as the indoor, both at Portland and

Dartmoor. I have no doubt that the same remark applies to all the stations, but I will only speak of what is within my personal knowledge. The celebrated moor upon which Dartmoor prison stands consists of bog-land stretching in one direction some twelve or fourteen miles, and in the front of the prison for four or five miles. The Government have had at their command the labour of at least five hundred men, not counting those employed at indoor labour, for the last forty years—more than sufficient time, with only ordinary industry, to have brought the whole of Dartmoor into a state of cultivation, and to have added greatly to the productive land of the country.

The moor only requires draining and trenching to make it "blossom like the rose," yet, with the exception of a few hundred acres in the immediate vicinity of the prison, it remains a barren and dreary morass. That it might be made profitable is placed beyond a doubt, because in a few acres immediately adjoining the prison asparagus, peas, rhubarb, and all the other luxuries of the garden, are brought to great perfection for the tables of governor and chaplain. Having provided for the needs of the officials, the authorities have done nothing more to the small portion of bog they have reclaimed than to make it grow carrots so coarse and bad as to be scarcely fit for human food. There is also plenty of good granite-stone in the quarries at Dartmoor, but it is made no use of beyond what is needed for the repair or enlargement of the prison.

The fact is, that here, and I believe on all public works, time is "frittered" away. Nothing is done completely or properly, and there is no actual responsibility resting upon any officer to get work done. The only thing in which the authorities are systematic is in *wasting time*. One hour is wasted regularly every day at Dartmoor in absurd military marchings and counter-marchings, and useless formalities, before the men go to work. Then, from want of proper business management, I have often seen three or four hundred men kept waiting for fifteen or twenty minutes, because at the last moment it was discovered that one gang was short of an officer, or one officer was short of a musket, or that a sufficient number of picks and shovels, or barrows, had not been provided. When at last a start is made, and the convicts reach the scene of their labours, another quarter of an hour is wasted in waiting for the principal officer who has charge of the division. It is his duty to see that all the gangs have arrived at their respective stations before any can commence work: he then blows his whistle and they "fall to." To what? I will give an example.

I recollect the circumstances very well, because it was just before Good Friday, and during the useless labours of that afternoon, my thoughts travelled back to happy Christmas and Easter seasons of past years. I heard the vile oaths, and the disgusting and obscene language of my comrades, and I contrasted the scene and its surroundings, with my once happy home, where I was cheered and smiled upon by a bright angel who made me, I suppose, *too* happy. I could not help fancying that her sister angels away up in the dark blue, got jealous of the Elysium which she made for me on this planet, and that they pleaded with the Great Father to call her home that she might enhance their joys, and sing her sweet songs to them instead of to me. My loved one seemed to be beckoning to me through the clear ether on that winter afternoon, and my greatest sorrow at that moment, was not that all my happiness in this world had been shipwrecked, not even that I had disgraced myself, and condemned myself to the filthy companionship of thieves and murderers: no! my *real* sorrow was that I had no power to answer her summons, and to join her for evermore in that sweet spirit-land "where the weary are at rest."

I was recalled from my reverie by an order from the "screw" to "fall in." We were all marched, some twenty-four of us, to the other end of a large field, nearly half a mile off, to fetch a sledge with which to remove some stones from a bog-hole. Returning with the sledge we commenced the removal, and dragged the stones to one corner of the field. An hour thus slipped away, and the principal officer came his rounds.

The stones had not been placed where he wished, and we were ordered to transfer them to the gate at the entrance to the field. We did that, and then the afternoon was gone.

We were resuming our jackets to return to the prison, when the farm bailiff came along upon his pony. He thought the stones would be in the way where we had last placed them, and directed that to-morrow we should remove them to the next field.

The whole twenty-five men had not earned one ounce of the brown bread, nor one pint of the cocoa they were returning to make their supper on. They had certainly not contributed a fraction towards the wages of the officers who had charge of them; and they had *learned* nothing, except lessons in vice and infamy with which they had regaled each other in their journeys backwards and forwards over that field. O yes, I was forgetting one thing; they had received one further confirmation of a doctrine which was being preached to them over and over again, day after day, and which therefore they could never forget, but would carry out of prison with them as a " lesson for life," the doctrine that *time and labour are of no value.*

I do not suppose that the heads of the Convict Department really believe that this is a healthy gospel to preach to lazy thieves whom they desire to transform into honest and industrious men, but they nevertheless preach it incessantly, in every public-works' prison in the land. I recollect another afternoon not long afterwards, in the same gang, when, in consequence of the gross want of system and preparation for emergencies which prevails on all Government works, a poor wretch was, so far as the officials knew or cared,

> " Cut off, even in the blossoms of his sin;
> Unhousel'd, disappointed, unanel'd;
> No reckoning made, but sent to his account
> With all his imperfections on his head."

The gang were employed in clearing the earth from around some large stones that they might be loosened and removed. This man was in a trench which he had made around the stone; his two companions, who were re-convicted men and up to everything, perhaps scented danger; at all events they had deserted their post, and this man, a novice in crime as well as at the work upon which he was employed, was alone. The stone suddenly gave way, and crushed him to death against the rear of the trench which he had made. The officer in charge had paid no attention to what was going on, or, accustomed as he was to the work, he would have warned the man of his danger. When the accident took place, a quarter of an hour elapsed before ropes and jacks could be obtained to release the poor fellow. During this time his dying cries, which haunt me now, were, " Fetch the ropes!"—" Get the jack!"—" For God's sake, help me!" The life was crushed out of him; the spark had not fled when he was released, there was indeed a little flame, but it only fluttered. No doctor was sent for the moment the accident occurred, and nobody thought of sending to the prison, which was a mile and a half off, for a stretcher, until the stone had been removed. Three quarters of an hour more elapsed before it arrived; and during all that time, which seemed to me an age, the poor fellow's dying cries, and his ravings about the dear ones at home, were piteous indeed. He arrived at the infirmary alive, but only in time to die; and he died a victim to the imbecility and want of forethought which seem to characterize the whole department. Personally I should not have felt this incident so much, if this man had been one of the old professional criminals, who care for no living soul in the world but themselves, and are themselves only blotches upon the fair face of nature which one would be glad to see obliterated; but this poor fellow had wife and children who were very dear to him. He had often expressed to me his deep regret for the offence which had brought him to prison, and his firm determination to steer a straight course in the future. There were extenuating circumstances in his case, too, which his friends were at this very time preparing to lay before the Secretary of State. They were spared their pains; but I have good hopes that he was able to carry with him a very sincere repentance, which will plead eloquently for him before a Judge whose chief attribute is mercy.

Dartmoor is, I believe, the only one of the

existing prisons at which there will be any outdoor employ for convicts after 1883. The works at the other stations have all been completed. The Breakwater at Portland was finished a quarter of a century ago, and since then the work which has been done for the War Department has been, as I will show further on, of an utterly useless character. Upon the moors of Devon there is sufficient employment for the number of men stationed there for the next two hundred years if the work goes on as *rapidly* as it has done heretofore. Whether what is done, in the way it is done, is of much practical value is an open question; and I really think that the Government would find it pay to employ some reliable scientific man, and some thoroughly practical agriculturist, who could give an opinion about future operations. My view is only that of an ordinarily intelligent man; but I think that labour, time, and money are being uselessly squandered.

I am quite sure that all that the land is at present made to produce could be purchased in the market for less money than it now costs, leaving the labour employed altogether out of the question, and reckoning it as wasted, which it certainly is. I have lately conversed with some practical men who are well acquainted with Dartmoor and its capacities. They are unanimous in thinking that with thorough draining the whole moor might be converted into magnificent pasture lands of inestimable value. I can testify that all the work now done towards draining the land is executed so carelessly and recklessly that it is very ineffective. I have seen miles of drain-pipes laid and covered in, which could not be other than inoperative, unless—as is not often the case—the laws of nature were suspended or reversed. All that the officers in charge care for, is to get so many feet of piping laid down for the governor's inspection. Whether the drains ever do drain the land, is no affair of theirs.

At Portland there *is* a little good stone-dressing done. During the year 1877 a great many stones were sent away to Borstal, near Chatham, and also to some works in progress at Sunningdale, but there is such a lack of earnestness and business management in the work that had the stones been charged for according to the time expended upon them, and at the rate of wages paid to a free stone-dresser, the contractor would have been compelled to add twenty-five per cent. to his price in order to avoid loss. Labour is considered of no value upon "public works," and when sales are made of stones dressed by convicts, the amount they have cost the Government in food and clothing for the prisoners, and the wages of the men who watch them, is not taken into consideration at all; if it were, the prices would be so high that no sales could be effected.

It is no exaggeration to say that an industrious free stone-mason would do as much work in an hour as a convict at Portland performs in a day. There is no task; a man may take a month over a stone 3 feet by 2 feet if he chooses, so long as he gives the officer in charge of him no trouble. There is one very large stone-dressing party who work close to the prison gates; a year and a half ago it comprised nearly eighty men, many of them being desperate characters, or men with very long sentences, whom it was not thought prudent to send far away from the prison; taking the party altogether it was composed of men who should have been made to work hard, and they were employed upon work which with ordinary good management, combined with industry, should have been remunerative.

What is the fact? Why this, that putting the very lowest market price upon the time occupied in the preparation of the stones, each stone cost the Government considerably more than double the price for which it was sold. A year's work by these eighty men would have been done by the same number of hands in an ordinary stonemason's yard certainly within a month. Free men working as leisurely as convicts are allowed to work in the stoneyards at Portland, could not possibly earn their bread; and with such habits engendered in prison, what right have the Government to suppose that when prisoners are discharged, they will be false to their prison training, and suddenly become possessed of habits of industry, which will enable them to be honest?

The work upon which the *majority* of the convicts at Portland are employed is still less profitable. It is not only the *total loss* of the labour of hundreds of men who are maintained at great expense by the Government, but it involves an immense outlay of the funds voted for the use of the War Department.

For many years a corps of engineers and one or two batteries of artillery have been stationed at Portland barracks. I am quite in accord with the truth when I say that for the last twenty years, the labour of 500 convicts has been wasted upon the Bill of Portland; wasted in providing practice for the engineer corps, and amusement for the artillery branch of the service. The real cost of convicts to the country is never known, because a charge for their labour is made by the Convict Department on the War Department, and is smuggled into the Army estimates.

While I was at Portland, racquet-courts and billiard-rooms were built by convicts for the convenience and pleasure of army officers, and ornamental grounds laid out for croquet and cricket. An ordinary contractor would have completed these works in one-fifth of the time that was occupied by the convicts, and with less than one-fifth the number of men. But this is the least portion of the corruption which exists. For twenty years the convicts have been building *ornamental* batteries, which surely can be of no earthly use as coast defences. With such carelessness are they constructed, that I have seen the same work done over again in three successive years, and batteries that have resisted the weather for two seasons I have seen pulled down and re-erected at a different angle to suit the whim of some new-fledged engineer.

I have seen a hundred men employed for weeks on barrow-runs, destroying a hill, and wheeling away the earth to fill up a valley a quarter of a mile away; the very next summer the engineer officer discovered that a mistake had been made, and that the earth must be carried back again; and this sort of thing has been going on for the last twenty years.

I was myself one of a party engaged for six months in excavating and wheeling away earth to a distance of about 300 yards. We then built some slopes and embankments, and built them so carelessly and badly, that a heavy shower at night often destroyed the work of the day. After a few more months the work was completed and looked a little "ship-shape." The captain of engineers came round with his theodolite to inspect the works, and discovered that the angles were altogether wrong. When I left Portland in January, 1878, a hundred or two of convicts were employed in doing all the work over again. It is the opinion of many of the officers who have charge of the labour, that these mistakes of the engineer corps are intentional, and simply designed to provide labour for the convicts. I beg leave to suggest that they are very expensive means to adopt, and that it is rather too bad to call upon the taxpayers, not only to support convicts who earn no part of their subsistence, but to lavish large sums in providing occupation and amusement for them.

It is not my business here to discuss the propriety of erecting *ornamental* batteries along the south coast, but I am satisfied that if during the recess some Members of Parliament would take the trouble to visit and inspect the coast defences upon the Bill of Portland, they would come to the same conclusion at which I arrived, viz., that half a dozen of the guns used in modern naval warfare would in half a dozen hours blow the so-called coast defences into smithereens.

The truth of my statements about the way in which work is performed can be easily proved, if some Member will move in the House of Commons for a return of the works executed by convicts for the War Department at Portland during the period named; the cost of the labour, and of the implements and material incidental to the labour; together with the expenses of the engineers and artillerymen engaged in superintending it. When this return has been made, let some honest Commissioner go down and see what the War Department have got to show for their money. I am told that these strictures would apply equally well to Portsmouth and to Chatham, but I have only spoken of what I have seen with my own eyes, and what, if allowed the opportunity, I could prove before a Committee of the House of Commons. I am guilty of no exaggeration when I say that two-thirds of the convicts are maintained at great expense to the country, and yield nothing in return, and that this result is the consequence of bad management and a corrupt system.

CHAPTER IV.

PRISON LIFE—CONVICTS AND THEIR GUARDIANS.

IT is my intention to make this chapter a desultory one. I want to convey to my readers some idea of the character of the average prison-warder, and I wish to relate a few remembrances of *eminent* criminals with whom I came in contact. I think the object I have in view—a reform of the present system—will be best served if I talk about the prisoners and officers in the same connection.

Immediately after conviction, all convicts in England, Scotland, and Wales are sent to what are called "separate prisons," in which they are detained for nine months to undergo their "probation." Roman Catholics are confined in Millbank Prison for this purpose; associates of the Church of England and other Protestants go to Pentonville.

In these *separate prisons*, and during the nine

months of probation, convicts are supposed to be governed under the *silent system*. I have no doubt that, even to-day, the directors of her Majesty's convict prisons—good, innocent, useless men—imagine that their regulations are carried out.

I had not been in the prison twenty-four hours ere I discovered that Sir Robert Walpole's doctrine, if not absolutely true, would not find many exceptions amongst prison warders. Certainly every second man " had his price."

At Pentonville the warder has sole charge of what is called a " landing," or floor, and this includes, I think, about forty prisoners. On this landing the warder is supreme; he distributes the food and the work, and if things go smoothly he is not interfered with, or visited by the principal or chief warder more than once in a week. He knows at what hour the Governor or Deputy-Governor may be expected to " walk his rounds," and then, of course, everything is in apple-pie order. At the end of each landing there is a closet and store-room. Only one prisoner is supposed to be there at a time; and if two prisoners are out of their cells at the same time for cleaning purposes the officer is supposed to take especial care that they hold no communication with each other. This is the theory. What is the practice? Well, that depends upon the amount of the fee you can give the warder. The British Government is not an economical one, but it is often economical in the wrong place. In the Convict Department it gives small salaries and imposes great responsibilities. It engages indigent and ignorant men without any high moral qualities, and the result is corruption and "malfeasance in office."

When I was at Pentonville I had a dear friend, since, alas, for me! gone to another world. He was to me faithful amongst the faithless. My folly did not alienate his great heart. Perhaps he knew, what I hope was true, that I was not *all* bad, and that, even after so disastrous a fall, penitence would come, and conscience would be roused, and I should "rise again" into a life of purity and honour. At all events, he stuck to me and visited me in prison when I was deserted by everybody else.

I very soon discovered that it was possible to communicate with him and yet elude the scrutiny of the Governor's office over my letters. I am quite conscious now, that in availing myself of the services of corrupt officials, I was guilty of a wrongful act, and which I now sincerely regret; but only those who have been deprived of communication with all in the world that they hold dear, can understand how great is the temptation in this matter to break the rules whenever an opportunity presents itself. As a result of my first letter by this "underground railway," my friend called at the house of the corrupt, but, to me, useful warder. The next morning I had the daily papers with my breakfast; the same evening I had my *Pall Mall* with my supper; and they *were* breakfasts and suppers, for I was supplied with dainties and luxuries which had no place in the "bill of fare" of her Majesty's prison.

This continued during the whole of the nine months of my stay at Pentonville. On my removal to Brixton, where I only stayed seven weeks, I could have made equally favourable arrangements, but sickness had laid hold of my friend, and before I left Brixton he was dead. To return to Pentonville: this Mr. Warder had, to my knowledge, half-a-dozen other clients upon his landing, so that he was able to double his salary at the very least. At the Christmas of 1873 my friend took him a large turkey, a sirloin of beef, puddings, pies, &c., which not only fed me, but regaled his family for a fortnight. Other privileges resulted from the feeing. I was installed in office as an "orderly." Instead of passing the weary hours, when I could obtain no readable book, in the solitude of my cell, I whiled away a large portion of my time in the store-closet, in conversation with other "paying prisoners," the warder himself keeping watch at the staircase, to give the "office" in case of the approach of visitors.

Here I made the acquaintance of two clergymen of the English Church who were, of course, men of intelligence and education, and with whom it was a pleasure to converse. One of them, I fear, was in prison not for the first time, the other had been convicted of forging some stock of an insurance company of which he was a director. His version of his downfall was naturally a very plausible one, but it was very apparent to me that he had been anxious to obtain a larger share of "loaves and fishes" than he could legally claim. His reverence had evidently a great liking for old port, and many a bottle of that gouty beverage used to find its way from his cellar in Yorkshire to Pentonville prison.

I met both these clergymen afterwards at Portland. The first-named, an Irishman, lost nearly the whole of his remission by infractions of the prison rules, trafficking in tobacco, and other little peccadilloes of that sort. The Yorkshireman was more canny; he kept himself straight, made friends with the doctor, was invalided, and transferred to Woking. I must say he was the jolliest-looking *invalid* I ever came across.

Another of my associates on this landing was a man for whom I felt a very deep sympathy. He bribed the warder, but it was for no other purpose than to obtain more frequent news of his wife, to whom he was devotedly attached, and who was wasting away of consumption. He had graduated at Oxford, and had achieved some success in his profession; but an absurd desire for display, and an ambition to keep as liberal a table and as well-bred horses as his richer neighbours, had led him into difficulties, from which he sought to extricate himself by forgery. His act and the folly which led up to it could not be apologized for; but then I was also a sinner, and I sympathized with the man when I saw what agony he suffered in the knowledge that his loved wife was dying, and that he could not be near to comfort her. No doubt, the conviction of her husband hastened the poor young wife's end.

One morning,—I think it was in September 1873,—the poor fellow was summoned into the presence of the Governor. I will describe the interview, because it portrays the character of the Governor. I know that he had many rough characters to control, who require rough treatment. At times, no doubt, he did well to be stern; but there are times when even the governor of a prison should unbend, and when sternness degenerates into brutality. This Governor was a militia or volunteer officer, and so, of course, stood severely on his military dignity; he insisted upon a salute from everybody, officers and prisoners, whenever he made his appearance.

On this September morning my sorrowing neighbour had been greatly disappointed at getting no news of his wife through the warder. At noon he was ushered into the awful presence of the Governor. He was in a nervous state, and not thinking much of military tactics, when the stern voice of the chief warder called out,—

"'Ands by your side! Hies to your front!"

GOVERNOR.—" Do you know a Mrs. Warner?"

PRISONER.—" Yes, sir."

GOVERNOR.—" Who is she? a relative?"

PRISONER.—" She is a friend with whom my wife is staying, and she is kindly nurs——"

GOVERNOR.—" That will do. There is bad news for you. Your wife is *dead*."

CHIEF WARDER.—" Right about face! March!"

At Portland and at Dartmoor, if any such event occurred, it was customary for the governor to authorize the chaplain to communicate the news privately to the prisoner in his cell, and I think it would have been more humane if the same course had been pursued at Pentonville.

I have given a specimen of prison officials, high and low, at Pentonville, and now let us go to Portland.

The change seemed at first an unfortunate one for me. The doctor passed me as suited for ordinary hard labour. All the previous physical exercise of which I had partaken had been for amusement. I once won the silver sculls in a sculling match at Henley; I had taken some tolerably rough horse exercise in my time in different parts of the world; and I could handle a rifle as well as most civilians; but up to now I had been a total stranger to the pick and shovel, and to the wheelbarrow.

I made no demur. I did not attempt to cant myself into the chaplain's good graces and get myself made a tailor; I did not follow the example of scores of great strong lazy fellows whom I saw around me, men who had never been accustomed to the refinements or even comforts of life, men who had come from the kennel and the dungheap, but who nevertheless from sheer laziness went crying day by day to the doctor, and at last bored him into a certificate for "light labour."

I went to work with a good heart. I knew that by my own folly and wickedness I had degraded myself to a convict's life, and I resolved to make the best of it and try to do my duty. I took my pick and shovel and became an "excavator." The work required of convicts on a barrow-run at Portland is, I should think, to a man at all accustomed to the labour, mere amusement. I worked at it for four months, and then I had to give in; but this was not because too much work was required of me. The continual stooping, which was new to me, certainly sent me home twice a day with a pain in my back; but the strain upon me, which reduced me rapidly from twelve stone to nine, was mental, and was not chargeable to my work.

It was in the summer of 1874, on a bright warm day, that I had to succumb. I could scarcely walk back to the prison in the dinner-hour; I was led down to the infirmary, and soon found myself under the penetrating eye of the assistant-surgeon, Dr. Bernard. As this gentleman was afterwards made a scapegoat in a case where a prisoner was supposed to have died through neglect, I will say what I know about him and about doctors generally in the service.

The duties of a medical officer in a convict prison are not only very responsible and arduous, but very difficult to perform. I recollect that during a considerable portion of last year, out of about 1,000 men at Dartmoor, 150 applied to see the doctor every day. I speak entirely of my own knowledge and from information gained from the men themselves, when I say that certainly 100 out of the 150, had nothing on earth the matter with them, and had they been free men, would no more have thought of going to the doctor, than they would of going to church. With some prisoners it is merely a mania; they will do anything, take anything, or go anywhere for variety.

Another large class, and not at all an insignificant percentage of the whole, actually trouble the medical officer, utter a lying complaint, and take a dose of medicine, for no other purpose than to get near a "pal" who has also arranged to be on the doctor's list. The object is to do a little stroke of business. A prisoner whose labour is out of doors can get a little piece of tobacco from an officer, if the prisoner who works indoors can give him in exchange some needles or some thread, or a piece of cloth, or a piece of leather, with which the aforementioned officer can mend his boots, or some boot-laces. The articles named are of course stolen from the tailors' and shoemakers' shops, and the exchanges are frequently made during the medical officer's visit, and whilst the prisoners are waiting their turn to see him.

Then there is another class of prisoners who, without the slightest reason, complain day after day for weeks of "extreme weakness," and "fainting sensations." Their hope and their object is to worry the doctor into ordering them a daily dose of cod-liver oil. They often succeed; the doctor having no time to go into detail, and feeling that it is better for him to err on the side of humanity. I knew scores of men, both at Portland and Dartmoor, who were for months taking tonics and cod-liver oil, who had nothing on earth the matter with them, and who used to chuckle to their pals over their success in hoodwinking the "croker."

There is another large class of prisoners who systematically "fake" themselves, as they call it; and unless the medical officer is a man of great experience, or a very shrewd fellow, he is often taken in. I knew one strong, hearty, lazy young fellow at Portland, who was able in some way to produce blood, and to deceive the medical officer, Dr. Askham, with the notion that his lungs were in a bad state. I am tolerably sure that the doctor doubted the fellow, but being uncertain, gave him the benefit of the doubt. The consequence was, that he was employed at the lightest kind of labour, and at last transferred to Woking, where I have no doubt he finished his very easy lagging. This young rascal took good care to complain at all times to Dr. Askham; he avoided the assistant medical officer, Dr. Bernard, who was too sharp for him, and for a great many more of the scamps.

I knew another man, a man of some education too, and who ought to have known better—a man who, by-the-by, had been a clerk in the Convict Department. He had been sentenced to five years for some swindling in connection with it. He was a great, strong, powerful fellow, as well able to do a day's work as any man on Portland Bill. His habit was to eat common soda, which he used to obtain from the men employed in the washhouse, and which he used to pay for with tobacco obtained from an officer. With this soda he was able to produce some effect which deceived Dr. Askham, and he was kept upon the lightest description of labour during his whole sentence, and was, when discharged, as fat as a porpoise.

Another deception practised to a very great extent is produced by the eating of soap. The action of the heart is very much influenced by it, and scores of men sneak into the infirmary, or evade their labour, by using it. It is also well known that quite a number of prisoners resort to more violent means to avoid labour, disabling themselves in an endless variety of ways.

With the knowledge of all these facts, it is

certainly the duty of medical officers in the convict prisons to keep a sharp look-out; and, as I have said, it is of immense importance that they should be men of experience and shrewdness, otherwise there is a great danger that in their determination not to be "done," they may sometimes refuse treatment where it is really required. Quite at the beginning of this year Dr. Harrison, who was assistant medical officer at Dartmoor, obtained his well-earned promotion, and was transferred to Wormwood Scrubs. Dr. Harrison was the most painstaking and careful man I saw in the service. If he erred, it was always on the side of humanity, and he certainly never refused treatment where it was needed; and yet this man was called a butcher and a murderer by some of the scoundrels who could not practise upon him.

In the spring of this year, and after my discharge, a green young doctor was sent to Dartmoor on probation, who evidently did not intend to be "done," but he was *too* smart. He lacked experience, and so was taken in by sharpers, and neglected men who really required treatment.

On the 21st of last June I received a letter by *Underground Railway* from a prisoner of some education who has no love for sharpers or habitual criminals, and whose word may be taken. He writes, "Dr. Power has been transferred to Portsmouth, and we have had here in his place"—well, I will leave out the name and my correspondent's rather violent description of the doctor. He proceeds, "He emptied the infirmary of all the sick men, and kept in, and pampered, all the sham lunatics and the fellows who were 'putting the stick on.' Let two instances of his treatment suffice. B 1183, James McDermot, had been complaining daily, for months, of yellow jaundice. Upon one occasion he fell out of the ranks of his party, when proceeding to work, for the purpose of seeing the doctor. The doctor told him there was nothing the matter with him, and that if he troubled him again he would send him to the punishment-cells. At length, when no longer able to walk, he did trouble him again, and was admitted to the infirmary; but it was too late, for after three weeks' infirmary treatment he was buried. In another instance, Leon Hendy, a

Frenchman, considered the best tradesman in the carpenter's shop, complained daily, but could get no treatment. In the meantime Dr. Smalley was appointed to this post. As soon as he arrived, he admitted Hendy at once, and did his best for him; but it was too late, he had been neglected too long, and in eight days he was dead."

I have quoted this letter, but I do not wish to convey the impression that these things often occur. They do not. It is the doctors who are "done" in the majority of cases, *not* the prisoners; but in order that the schemes of impostors may be as much as possible frustrated, and that on the other hand really necessitous cases should receive attention, I think I am justified in urging upon the Directors the importance of appointing only such men as are shrewd and skilful. In justice to them I ought to state that the man who made these blunders at Dartmoor, and who was on probation for the post of Assistant Medical Officer, was *not* appointed.

Let me now go back to my own experience

at Portland, and to Dr. Bernard. The moment he saw me, and scarcely asking me a question, he gave the order, "Put that man to bed." In bed I remained for five or six weeks, receiving from Dr. Bernard the best possible treatment, as much nourishing food as I could take, and constant attention from him daily. This was in 1874; and from that time until the hour of my release I never had to lay up for a day. Dr. Bernard made a man of me, and I went again to outdoor labour and continued at it until my removal to Dartmoor in 1878.

I have said that Dr. Bernard was dismissed the service on account of his supposed neglect of a prisoner who died. The facts are, that the coroner's jury made some ugly remarks, and it became necessary that there should be a victim. Why it should have been the *assistant* medical officer who was made responsible I never understood; but it seems that the chief medical officer, who was a very uncertain man, and acted upon impulses, which were sometimes generous and sometimes otherwise, had brought the man some champagne from his own cellar the day before his death. This act seems to have convinced the ignorant jurymen that the medical officer could not have been at fault, and so the assistant became the victim. My observation convinced me that if a prisoner was *really* ill he always got treatment, and *skilful* treatment, from Dr. Bernard, but he was the very deuce at unearthing tricksters and schemers. The man who died had been a trickster for years, and at last made himself really ill. Dr. Bernard, knowing his character, perhaps took little interest in the case; and really, I think men who act in this way have no right to expect much consideration from doctors when they are indeed ill. Knowing that men have been " faking " themselves for years, it is no wonder if a doctor, after he has found them out, gives little heed to what they say.

I watched Dr. Bernard very closely, for the simple reason that I used to hear all the schemers and habitual thieves abuse him, and whilst I admit that he was sharp and severe with tricksters, his treatment of men who were really ill was skilful and kind.

CHAPTER V.

CONVICTS AND THEIR GUARDIANS (*continued*).

THE first prisoner whose acquaintance I made in the infirmary at Portland was the noted forger, William Roupell, formerly M.P. for Lambeth. He was head nurse and doctor's factotum, and a nice easy time he seemed to have been having during the greater part of his lagging.

Now, while I am so strongly of opinion that there should be a classification of prisoners, I hold that it is manifestly unjust and unfair that any partiality should be shown to a prisoner on account of his former social position, or because he may have influential friends to whisper into a Director's ear. That Roupell had such friends, and that great partiality was shown to him, was too patent to escape observation, and when one reflects upon the enormity of his crime, I think that any exceptional leniency in his favour was scarcely justifiable. I found Roupell a tolerably intelligent man, but not particularly so. I think I shall do him no injustice when I say that most of his reading was done after his conviction. He had a good deal of cunning, but the little knowledge he possessed was very superficial, and he impressed me with the idea that surely it could have been nothing but ready-money and beer which deluded the electors of Lambeth into supposing him to be a statesman.

I believe that his father had stood in the relation of "Uncle" for a great many years to the denizens of the classic thoroughfares which abut upon the Westminster Bridge Road; and as it was not then known that he had defrauded an elder brother of his inheritance, this family tie may have endeared him to his cousins in the New Cut; I rather incline, however, to the belief that it was *only* the beer which influenced the incorruptibles of Lambeth.

William Roupell told me that after finishing his "separates" he had been sent to Portsmouth, and had there been compelled to work in the "chain-cable gang" at the dockyard. "Fine work for a *gentleman*," he remarked, "polishing chains." I asked him if he were in good health, and he said, "Oh, yes; but I was not going to do that sort of thing." He had to do it, it seems, so long as he remained at that station, for Captain Harvey, the present estimable governor of Millbank Prison was then in command there, and he was not open to any outside influences. Roupell's friends could produce no effect upon Captain Harvey; he was treated with humanity and impartial justice, but with no favour.

As I was for a few days under the control of Captain Harvey prior to my discharge, and as I heard a great deal about him from both officers and prisoners, I take this opportunity of saying that I consider him a model governor. Strict justice is in his hands tempered by consideration and humanity, and I cannot help adding that he impressed me with the idea that he was one of the most perfect specimens of an English gentleman with whom I had ever come in contact.

I had occasion to speak to him almost on the eve of my discharge, and he volunteered a few words of good advice, in the spirit, and with a gentleness, which one would expect from a brother who was really anxious for one's true welfare. I felt sincerely grateful to him, and I shall always honour him.

William Roupell, finding that Captain Harvey was not to be tampered with, pulled another string. Through some influence brought to bear upon the Directors he was transferred to Portland, and his future path was strewn with roses. He was soon installed as head nurse in the infirmary. He had the good fortune to be convicted before the passing of the Act of 1864, so that he was entitled to a very different diet to that served out to the rest of the prisoners, a better diet, in fact, than can be regularly obtained by the best and most honest and sober of English mechanics.

Roupell, however, was not satisfied with that. By some means or other he had got on the blind side of governor and doctors, and there was no luxury ordered to any sick man which was not at the command of William Roupell. I tasted neither fish nor poultry, game nor fruit, for nearly six years, but I saw Roupell get such luxuries every day, and he never lacked port wine, bottled stout, and brandy. He had a nice little piece of garden given him in the infirmary grounds, and here he built himself a summer-house and a grotto, and he whiled away pleasant hours in tending his flowers.

In the afternoon he frequently went down to the governor's private office for an hour or two. What he did there I do not know of my own knowledge, but officers who had no interest in lying about the matter told me that he had access to the newspapers, and that his correspondence was unlimited. He made a great display of his piety. I thought it too lavish and obtrusive to be genuine; but I hope I was mistaken. The chaplains did not think so, and they ought to know better than myself. He stood high in *their* good graces, and indeed was "hail-fellow-well-met" with governors, doctors, and chaplains. To the schoolmasters and principal warders he assumed a patronising air. Altogether he had quite a jolly time of it, and was even better off than the late occupant of the Westminster Clock-tower, for his nights were not disturbed by the ticking or striking of either "Big Ben" or his "grandfather's clock."

I made the acquaintance of another prisoner who claimed to have been born with a silver spoon in his mouth, and as what I have to say about him will necessitate the revelation of a remarkable instance of the corruptibility of prison officials, it may be considered germane to my purpose. Now, although I think that with one slight alteration the present prison diet would be a sufficient and wholesome one, it certainly is not, and *ought* not to be, a *fattening* one.

The moment I saw "Mr. Vane" I was convinced that he had "other resources," for he was in splendid condition. He was of large physique, and would naturally require a little more food than some, but his proportions were grand, and he looked as well-fed as any Lord Mayor. This Vane was not a good-looking man, and certainly bore no personal resemblance to the Vane-Tempests; but he had plausible manners, and by dint of hard lying and fictitious letters from a woman outside who addressed him by that name, he had induced the chaplain, doctor, and Scripture-reader to believe that he was Lord Ernest Vane-Tempest. He so imposed upon the credulity of a kindhearted old clergyman who sometimes visited the prison, that the good old dupe parted with some considerable sum of money for the purpose of aiding a woman with whom the convict had lived, and whom he said he had privately married. His story was that he had hidden his real position at the time of his conviction, to shield his family from disgrace, and that they were still ignorant of his downfall, and supposed him to be in America. Consideration for the family doubtless prevented the authorities from making inquiries, but I fancy the governor always doubted the story.

The real Lord Ernest Vane-Tempest had in his youthful days cow-hided a brother officer in the Haymarket. To avoid arrest Lord Ernest went to America, and during the Civil War served as an aide on the staff of General McClellan. On his return to England he was pursued by his enemy, and was imprisoned for a short time as a first-class misdemeanant. This youthful escapade gave a sort of colour to the impostor's tale, and his weak-minded dupes swallowed it on the "Give-a-dog-a-bad-name-and-hang-him" principle.

The real Lord Ernest is now, and always was, a man of high honour, and unless the "sprees" of his minority are to be quoted against him still, has through his life maintained the reputation of a gentleman. I told the chaplain on one occasion that this fellow was not Lord Ernest; for that I had seen and known that nobleman, but as he seemed to think I was mistaken I troubled no more about it.

One day the party to which I was at the time attached were called to assist No. 27 party, in which Vane was to load some stones. I made an excuse to get near him, and addressed him thus: "Mr. Vane, I think." "Yes, I am." "Do you know Lord Ernest Vane-Tempest?" "Well, yes, I should think so; do you not know who I am?" "No, I cannot say that I do; but I know Lord Ernest Vane-Tempest, and he and I have frequently breakfasted together at Wil-

H

lard's Hotel in Washington." This Vane gave me a wide berth afterwards; indeed, he was in a few weeks discharged. What I learned afterwards from the officer who provided him with his aldermanic fare, shows that these constitutional thieves do their best to "keep their hands in," even in prison. This rascal succeeded in his rogueries.

I think it was in the summer of 1876 that I, amongst others, was drafted into a party which worked some "trawleys" on the incline leading down to the Breakwater. I soon found that the officer in charge was what prisoners call a "square man," that is, a man who could be squared. He was an Irishman, had been a colour-serjeant in the Infantry, was decorated with four or five medals, and was in receipt of a pension of some two shillings and threepence per day. It is not necessary to relate how I became intimate with him, but after awhile he told me the history of his connection with "Mr. Vane." Vane had thoroughly satisfied this man that he was Lord Ernest, that upon his release he would obtain possession of an estate, and that in return for the services rendered to him in prison he would appoint this officer his steward, with a house and salary of two hundred per annum.

In addition to these great promises, he also gave the "screw" a promissory-note for two hundred pounds, at the foot of which he forged the name of Lord Ernest Vane-Tempest, and which note I afterwards had in my hand. On the strength of this the corrupt official furnished this scoundrel with tobacco day after day for *two* years. There were two other prisoners, tools of Vane's, in the secret; the tobacco was planted in certain places upon the works, and carried into the prison and exchanged for the beef and mutton upon which Mr. Vane got so fat.

So satisfied was the officer that he had got hold of a good thing, that when Vane was discharged, he, not having sufficient money, pawned his watch in order that his Lordship might have a fashionable suit of clothes in which to go home and "take possession of his estates." Not hearing from his Lordship according to promise, the "screw" got leave of absence, and made a visit to Plymouth to look up his Lordship. He did not find him at the fashionable address he expected, but after some trouble he unearthed him in a low lodging-house, at which, he assured me, he would not have stayed himself. "The gaff was blown" now, but the swindler was safe; he knew that the "screw" could not prosecute him for forgery without criminating himself.

This corrupt officer, who is only a sample of plenty more at Portland and proportionate numbers at other stations, had several irons in the fire in 1876, and was trying to make up his Vane losses. He was bleeding the family of a young man from Leicester, whose friends were well off, and he did this under pretence of accommodating, the prisoner with luxuries. But one of his acts was such a flagrant robbery that, although, for the sake of a young lady of good position who is implicated, the fellow cannot be prosecuted, I think it my duty to expose it for two reasons: one is, that it may incite the Directors of the Convict Department to keep a sharper eye on these rascals; and the other is that it may prevent persons of respectability, who may be unfortunate enough to have a relation in prison, from becoming the victims of these harpies.

A man of good family committed an offence in 1873 which sent him into penal servitude. His family deserted him, but a young lady, herself the niece of the governor of a London prison, and to whom the man was betrothed, visited him in the House of Detention without the knowledge or consent of her relatives. Up to the time of his conviction she supplied him with such luxuries as he wished, carrying them to the prison daily with her own hands. After his conviction and removal to a convict prison she cheered him by her letters. The prisoner became acquainted at Portland with the "square warder" in question. He had sufficient honour not to desire to tax his lady-love to send him luxuries; but he knew that she would gladly pay for more frequent correspondence, and he made arrangements with the "screw." For some time the letters came, then they failed. They failed, because in them the young lady spoke of having sent money to procure him luxuries. When the prisoner was discharged, he found that his lady-love had parted with a considerable sum of money to this fellow under the delusion that she was ministering to the comfort and happiness of her lover.

For aught I know this officer is still in the service, and perhaps still fattening on the proceeds of other knaveries.

In the exercise-yard at Portland one Sunday I made the acquaintance of a prisoner, whom I mentioned incidentally in another chapter. He was educated for the priesthood of the Catholic Church, and was therefore a man of some culture; but his propensities were so thoroughly immoral, and his intentions for the future, as detailed to me, are of so dangerous a character, that he will require to keep a sharp look-out or he will find more "breakers ahead."

He was a good-looking man, with exceedingly plausible manners; and, I should think, about forty years of age. But although good-looking and agreeable in his manners, he always reminded me of Bulwer Lytton's " Candid Man." He was too frank, too familiar, too *dégagé* to be perfectly natural, and he had a sly and cunning expression in his perverse and vigilant eye which used to make me shudder.

It may be recollected that this fellow had by taking fashionable lodgings in Mayfair and sporting a brougham induced a West-End jeweller to send for his wife's inspection three or four thousand pounds' worth of jewellery. With the assistance of his wife he drugged the man with chloroform, and, leaving him asleep, took the diamonds, made good his escape into Holland, and disposed of the greater part of them. The wife was arrested, but acquitted on the ground that she acted under the influence of her husband. When a few months had elapsed he ventured back into England to call for his wife, intending to embark with her for "Dixie's Land." His wife had been watched; he was "trapped," and sentenced to eight years' penal servitude. He played his cards very well at Portland, had an easy time of it, and was a strong, healthy-looking fellow when discharged. From his own admissions to me he lived in clover in London for many years, and secured a good income from the proceeds of bogus advertisements in the London *Times*.

As I notice advertisements every day in the leading papers, which I have no doubt are spurious, I presume that this class of thieves still find "gulls." Here is a sample of this prisoner's many devices, dictated by his own lips :—

"The captain of a steamship, trading to Brazil, has been instructed by a wealthy nobleman of that country to obtain for him a first-class governess for his children. She must be familiar with the Spanish language, and thoroughly competent to instruct in English, French, and music. To a competent person the nobleman is willing to pay the unusual salary of £400 a year, together with board, lodging, and first-class travelling expenses. Applications must be accompanied by complete and minute testimonials, and addressed to Captain ———, Southampton-street, Strand, London."

To this tempting advertisement he received nearly two hundred replies from all parts of the United Kingdom and the Continent. To each one he gave the same answer,—She was one of the fortunate three whom he had selected from a host of applicants, and whose testimonials he had determined to forward to Brazil, casting the onus of final selection on the nobleman himself. The postage of the testimonials to Brazil would cost about 10$s.$ 6$d.$; and if that amount were forwarded by return of post, the package would go out by the next mail. He assured me that more than a hundred fools were green enough to fall into his trap.

This is, of course, but a sample of his multitudinous schemes. His intention when discharged was to go to New York, and he informed me that he had perfected a scheme which would defy detection, and by which he intended to make a fortune out of New York bankers. I sincerely hope that Brother Jonathan will be too "smart" for him.

I suppose it is useless to caution the public against bogus advertisements, they having been warned again and again. If a situation is offered on the condition of the deposit or payment of a sum of money, no doubt a swindle is intended. If a man who wants to lend money is anxious first of all to handle the money of the borrower, no doubt he is a swindler. If a very first-class piano is offered for sale at a very low price by a lone widow requiring immediate funds, it may be set down as a swindle. If a person "in misfortune" desires to dispose of the duplicates of valuable jewellery which has been pledged for a quarter of its value, the person "in misfortune" is a sure swindler.

I have unfortunately had to live amongst swindlers for six years, and have heard of a great many of their tricks. One mean little swindler told me that he made a fair living for some time by inserting cheap advertisements of a tempting character in the *Clerkenwell News* requiring that a *stamp should be enclosed for reply*. Of course no reply was ever sent.

I came in contact at Portland, in 1874, with *Hill,* one of the Yankee "skallewags" who aided that clever engraver and "cannie Scot," Macgregor, in the gigantic forgeries on the Bank of England. Hill asserts that he was a mere clerk to Macgregor and the Bidwells, and seems to have hopes that his friends will yet succeed in getting an alteration of his sentence. He is a very good prisoner, and I think has never been reported. He has always been under a strict and special guard, and has been employed within the precincts of the prison, the authorities fearing a repetition of the attempts made in London. Hill has I am sure given up all idea of escape, and is doing his best to keep a good character, so that he may at least secure his freedom at the end of twenty years.

Last year, at Dartmoor, I came in contact with another of the party, the elder Bidwell. He has pursued entirely different tactics to Hill, and has given ten times more trouble to the authorities than any prisoner has ever done before. From the first he has steadily refused to use his legs, asserting that they are paralysed. As the doctors have used the batteries upon him several times, they know that it is all a fraud. Still he persists, and his legs are now no doubt stiffened from misuse. If he could be compelled to walk short distances at first, and then longer ones, he could speedily obtain the use of his limbs, but he is very obstinate; and if the authorities send him to the tailors' shop, or anywhere else to work, they have to put him on the back of another prisoner, and when he arrives there he refuses to work. He has had any amount of bread-and-water punishment, and has thoroughly deserved it, for in addition to his laziness and obstinacy, and imposture, his habits are of the most filthy and disgusting character. He is not likely to live to come out of prison again, but that is his own fault.

Apropos of swindles. I came in contact with a good many of the "cadger" class who had stepped over the cadging line and dropped into felony. I was very much amused with the story of an old brute named Chown, who came from Torquay. He did a little swindle upon that large-hearted, generous, and truly noble lady, the Baroness Burdett-Coutts. I have no doubt she is exposed to similar attacks every day. It was Christmas-time, and the Baroness was distributing her Christmas gifts. He called, and was awarded half-a-sovereign. Her ladyship asked the old rascal if he had a wife, and he was ready with his artful lie, and said that he had, and five children. He was told to send her up. He found a woman of bad character, took her up, and by a plausible and piteous tale obtained another half-sovereign, a piece of beef, two blankets and a cloak. I felt that I should like to wring the neck of the old vagabond when I heard him chuckle over the way in which he had done Lady "Cadet Boots," as he called her.

There were two or three beauties at work in the same party with this fellow. I recollect one contemptible hound who told me that he had not been at liberty for three weeks before he was again "lagged," and had not seen his wife or children. He said he was on the drink, and as he had cleared everything out of his home upon which he could raise sixpence at the pawnshop, he knew it was of no use to go there. His wife had been slaving to get bread for five children, and when he left his home he left it without a crust. He told the tale himself; of course he had no shame, or he would not have lived to tell it. He got up in the early morning and sneaked out of the house with his wife's boots, very indifferent ones, but the only ones in the family, and invaluable to her, for without them she could not go to her labour and get scant bread for the children of this drunken savage. Upon these boots he raised ninepence at the pawnbroker's, and spent it at the next tavern for gin.

This wretch was in the church choir at Portland, and took the Sacrament regularly. I wonder it did not choke him. I have heard him say that the first use he should make of his gratuity on his discharge would be to get a quart of beer and a quartern of gin, and in that, if in nothing else, I have no doubt he will keep his word. In the face of such evidence who can wonder at the earnestness and enthusiasm of Sir Wilfrid Lawson? I wish him God-speed with all my heart.

During the whole time of my imprisonment I kept my ears wide open to glean all that I could from criminals themselves about the causes of crime. I cannot avoid the conclusion that gin-palaces are but half-way houses on the road to a convict prison. In them the victim lays in fresh supplies, which help him to complete his journey.

If men would use their wits, and keep their heads cool, they would ascertain that, if they really desire to possess a good conscience, a peaceful home, and happiness in the future, there is no highway to these luxuries through the tavern or the gin-palace. If they will but open the eyes of their reason wide enough, they may see inscribed over the door of every gas-bedizened and flaunting gin-palace in the land this inscription, "No Thoroughfare to Honesty or Happiness."

This drink and tavern curse is not confined to the lower class. Let me give the instance of two young men whom I saw at Dartmoor. The first was in a mercantile house in the City. He became enamoured with one of the painted and powdered decoy-ducks who are on exhibition at the premises of a notorious publican within a mile of Regent Circus. At first he spent a shilling or two nightly; but he quickly found that the road to favour with his *inamorata* was a bottle of Moët, of which she and her painted sisters partook freely, very often a second bottle, and then a third. The acquaintance soon ripened; excited with the champagne, a diamond ring was promised, then an emerald, then ear-drops and a bracelet.

On Sunday a trap was hired, and this young man, who had a loving mother and sisters at home, and a virtuous young sweetheart who was breaking her loving heart over him, disported himself at Richmond in the company of a gin-drinking and beer-drawing harlot. He told me himself that, from the time he first went to that tavern he never went to bed perfectly sober, and that all his follies were committed under the influence of champagne. He at last robbed his employers in order to obtain money to supply this woman with dress and jewels and champagne, and he is now ruminating over his wickedness on the bogs of Dartmoor.

He had the mortification to learn from a friend, while awaiting his trial, that his *inamorata*, whom he supposed would be weeping over his downfall, used to sell his presents to keep a lazy, drunken husband, with whom she lived, after tavern hours, in a dingy lodging in Dean Street, Soho. He was also informed that his corner in the bar had already been filled up by another ninny, which ninny has probably by this time arrived at the same depôt.

The other fellow was one for whom I felt really sorry. At the time of his conviction he was on the eve of passing an examination for one of the learned professions; but he had been an *habitué* of the buffet of what I will call the "Royal Grill Room" Theatre, and a lounger at the stage-door of that celebrated establishment. He made the acquaintance of one of the "ladies of the ballet," a party whose mother probably lived in "Short's Gardens," or "Fullwood's Rents," and who had been taught to drink gin from her babyhood in the purlieus of Drury Lane.

The "young lady" had learned her lesson. When invited to supper she declined everything but "fizz." Her suppers and those of her lover often amounted to a sovereign and a half. She was so good a customer to the landlord that a good word was spoken for her to the manager; and, as her lover, under the influence of champagne, promised to provide for her the handsomest dress and boots that the costumier could provide, she was promoted to the front row of the ballet. Here, adorned by jewellery her lover had committed forgery to obtain, and set off to the best advantage by the dress, boots, and tights he had bought for her, she attracted the attention of the Hon. Arthur Numskull, of the Crutch and Toothpick brigade. She gave her old friend the cold shoulder at once, and he had the mortification to see her handed into the Hon. Arthur's brougham when the theatre closed. He went to the Royal Grill-room buffet and got drunk by himself that night. Going to his chamber in a maudlin state, he forgot to take some precaution which would have deferred the revelation of his crime, and about twelve the next day, and before he was sober, he was in Newgate.

These are stern, hard facts, and I learned them from the men themselves while under punishment, afflicted with remorse, and after they had had time calmly to reflect upon their conduct.

Of course entanglements with women of this

sort are always effected under the influence of liquor. A sober man who did such things would be sent by his friends to a lunatic asylum, and ought to be.

I have set these things down because I know that there are hundreds of young men in London travelling the same road. These lessons ought to warn them. They may take my word for it, a convict prison is a very hell to a man of any culture and refinement; herding with "Zulus" and "Yahoos" can be nothing to it; and after release worse still will be their fate: no character, no home, no friends, no employment. I say to them with all my heart, in the name of God, "turn up" taverns.

CHAPTER VI.

CONVICTS AND THEIR GUARDIANS: PRISON PUNISHMENTS, ETC.

THERE are a great number of what are called "confidence men" in convict prisons, and I think they invariably belong to the incorrigible class. Their assumption, in prison as well as out, and their unblushing impudence are unbounded. I met two of these fellows at Portland, and, as I have heard of them both since their release, it may be interesting to show that crime is, in some men, ingrained.

One of them had, I believe, really borne her Majesty's commission in early life. He called himself Captain Logan, and had served two terms of penal servitude. He always obtained the means of living when he happened to be free by sheer bounce and bravado. He obtained goods from credulous shopkeepers by seeming to take it for granted that he was known as a man of fortune and family, and that to doubt him was an unpardonable insult. He of course raised money upon everything he obtained at the nearest pawnbrokers. Now and then he overdid the thing and was " trapped."

The sentence which he finished while I was at Portland was, I think, one of twelve years, sufficient, one would imagine, to cure any man of ordinary intelligence or feeling. Not at all, as the sequel will show. In prison his great object seemed to be to earn the title of a "dare-devil." He set all prison rules at defiance, and treated the authorities with contempt. He never did any work, and so earned no remission. He was continually under punishment, and did 850 days of his sentence upon bread and water: at least, he was supposed to have done. The fact was, that during his whole sentence he had friends outside who were foolish enough, through corrupt officers, to supply him with the means of pampering his appetite. He was never without *tobacco*, and with tobacco he could purchase anything. I regret to say that with a large number of "screws" he was the most popular prisoner at the station. In the absence of the higher officials he simply did as he liked.

In the society of gentlemen, or educated men of ordinary acumen, this fellow would not have passed muster at all. Whatever may have been the respectability of his family, he was an ignorant, vulgar fellow. He sometimes would sneak up by my side at the Sunday exercise, but he always afflicted me with nausea. Still, he was wonderfully successful in imposing upon the unsophisticated and upon partially-educated men.

There was a fellow at Portland belonging to the middle class, a man of tolerable, but partial education. He was affianced to a young lady who had some property which was under her own control, and his only hope for the future was in marrying her, and, aided by her fortune, making a fresh start in some colony. He was so anxious to communicate with her, that he was weak enough to commission any tolerably-educated prisoner who was discharged to call upon her with messages.

I knew his weakness, and seeing him in close conversation with Logan one Sunday I warned him against the man. It was of no use, he was sure Logan was a "gentleman" and would not deceive him. He certainly did not deceive me. As I expected, his first act after arriving in London was to seek out the girl. He first obtained some money from her to "relieve the necessities of her friend in prison." After a little further acquaintance he told her that he felt so deep an interest in her that he could not help, for *her* sake, betraying his friend at Portland. He assured her that her lover had confided to him the secret that he did not care for her, but that marriage was his only chance. This led up to his real object. He did his best to entrap the poor girl into a marriage with himself. I am very happy to say that he not only failed in that, but that within a few weeks he was again convicted. My only regret is that the judge did not sentence him to three dozen.

I must briefly refer to another confidence man, because, by a remarkable coincidence, he obtained the confidence of this "lover" I have spoken of at Portland, and played almost precisely the same game with regard to the young lady that Logan had done.

This man I have referred to incidentally before; he was the promoter of bubble companies, and the associate of a "fishy" baronet who has been convicted of the same sort of thing. His great game was to obtain confidence by organizing banquets and testimonials in his own honour. Having received instructions from his fellow-prisoner he sought out the young lady as soon as he arrived in London. He told a very similar tale to the one concocted by Logan as to the lover's duplicity. He invented a lie as to his having been divorced from his wife, the real fact being that in justice to her own character the wife had been compelled to leave him. He then did his best to entrap the young lady into a bigamous marriage. He failed in this. I was describing him to a gentleman high in authority at Scotland-yard the other day, and he told me that he believed they had got him again. I hope he was not mistaken.

The "Claimant" had left Dartmoor for Portsmouth before my arrival at the former place. I heard a good deal about him of course. He seems to have given an infinity of trouble. His applications to address the Home Secretary, and to have interviews with Directors, governor, doctor, and priest were incessant. He got admitted to the church choir for two reasons,— he obtained a more comfortable seat, and he was excused labour on Saturday mornings that he might attend practice. The organist assured me that he had no notion of singing, and that the noise he made was something between the chirp of a crow and the croak of a raven.

It was generally admitted by the more intelligent prisoners who came in contact with him that his habits and manners were vulgar. He was doing his best, by the aid of French schoolbooks furnished him by the priest, to master the French language; and he made all sorts of promises to a prisoner who was in the next cell to him, and who could speak French, if he would aid him, but this man told me that he was very stupid at it, and that his progress was very slow.

When the Claimant first went to Dartmoor he seems to have had a good friend in the gentleman who was at that time governor of the prison. He was extremely troublesome, constantly breaking prison rules, and constantly being reported for doing so; but so long as the Major remained in command, he was never punished, and, when he received visits from his friend Dr. Kenealy and others, the visits took place, contrary to regulations, in the governor's office, and extra time was allowed him.

The advent of Captain Harris as governor was a misfortune for Castro or Orton, or whoever he may be. I may here take the opportunity of doing an act of simple justice to Captain Harris. I am quite sure that if the son or brother of the Secretary of State were a prisoner under his control, he would be treated with precisely the same indulgence as every other prisoner, and no more. The Claimant when next he received a visit did so behind the bars, and within the time specified by the rules. When reported for insolence he was sentenced to two days' bread-and-water, and he got a second punishment for the same offence and some others. By the doctor's orders he had 8 oz. of additional bread per day and 8 oz. of potatoes, and on meat and soup days he had increased rations.

I presume his friend Mr. Whalley worried the Home Secretary into having him transferred to Portsmouth, where, I am told, he is fetching a tolerably easy "lagging." Perhaps the air there is not so bracing, but at Dartmoor his appetite was enormous. I know men employed in the tailor's shop who did not need all their food, and who gave him some constantly; and the orderlies who carried round the bread were in the habit of yielding to his entreaties to shy him a loaf, if a "good screw" happened to be on duty. By the way, a "good screw," amongst prisoners, means a man who does *not* do his duty. I knew a little Irishman who told me that one day he was able to give the Claimant six six-ounce loaves, and that he came very near getting three days as a reward for his goodnature.

The big man was very unpopular with some of his neighbours, who say that he was a bad sleeper, and used to puff and blow, and grunt and groan all through the small hours. He was unpopular with the warders because it was with the greatest difficulty he could be got to scrub his cell, or keep his cell-furniture clean. But I won't say any more about the fellow. I should think the world has had enough of him, in all conscience.

Before turning from the prisoners to the officers, I will take the opportunity to warn benevolent and well-meaning religious people against the pretensions of prisoners, who, on their discharge, set up for converted characters, and seek to be employed in evangelization.

God forbid that I should deny the possibility of a man who has erred being truly penitent, and desirous of pursuing for the rest of his life a course of industry and honour. Such is, I hope, my own case, and I firmly believe that I have met with others who have determined that, come what will, their life shall for the future be one of inflexible integrity.

But when scamps who have been in and out of prison a score of times, and are so well known to the police that they can scarcely hope to escape detection if they continue their old practices, take up a new line in which to pursue their roguery, and try to cant themselves into the position of missionaries and Scripture-readers, they are surely not to be trusted. Whenever the missionary box or the "bag" is heavy enough they will play a Judas trick upon it. Sincere men will go honestly and quietly to earnest labour, and prove their faith by their works. I know a man who is at this moment in the tailor's shop at Dartmoor. He has ingratiated himself into the chaplain's favour by his assumed devotion, and by regularly partaking of the Sacrament. He has thoroughly made up his mind that when released he will adopt the "religious dodge," as he calls it. He says that he is sure, by pulling the right wires, he can knock a living out of pious dowagers by attempting the conversion of the bog-men of Connemara, or organizing a special mission for the thieves'-quarters in Sevendials or Kent-street. I am really afraid he could find dupes to aid him. If he wants a character or a recommendation, he shall have it now.

I conscientiously believe that if his aged

mother had but half-a-crown in the world, and was sleeping with it beneath her pillow for safety, and that he knew her bread for the next week depended on it, he would in the dead of night sneak out with it, await the opening of an early tavern, and remain until he had poured half-a-crown's worth of the decoction sold there down his villanous throat.

I am familiar with the history of the treachery of Judas, and how he sold his Master for thirty pieces of silver. After a long and involuntary intimacy with the habitual criminals of England, let me here register my firm conviction that the man of whom I speak, and the great majority of his associates in crime, would sell their own sister for a quartern of gin, if no higher price could be obtained.

Let me now have a say about the men at present employed as prison warders; and I shall speak of prison punishments in the same connection, because the two subjects are so inextricably connected. A very large proportion of them are discharged soldiers and sailors. Now I am quite conscious that army reform has greatly raised the moral status of soldiers during the last fifteen years, but is it not a fact, that twenty or twenty-five years ago the army was recruited chiefly from the dregs of the population, largely indeed from the very thief-class? Scarcely any man enlisted until he was barred from the ranks of decency.

At the time these men served the Crown in the army,—and indeed up to very recent times,—the barrack-room was a rookery of immorality and vice; and the men taken from such a source are not very likely to exercise a moralising influence upon prisoners? The Government takes the young offender,—"the first-timer," the novice in crime, the man of semi-respectability who has stumbled,—and it puts him between two hot fires, which I do not think are calculated to purify him. It gives him as companions and tutors the habitual criminals whose characters I have tried to describe, and it gives him as monitors and masters a set of beings whose morals are of the loosest, who have not the slightest respect for truth or honour, and whose every-day language is almost as filthy as that of the filthiest whom they are paid to control. I have spoken of their corruption. During my stay at Dartmoor two had to abscond to escape prosecution for felony, one was actually a principal warder, and was associated in his roguery by the chief clerk of the governor, who also absconded. Then in matters of honour and truthfulness, although, of course, there are many, very many, honourable exceptions, yet the rule is that the majority of officers will say anything before the governor, if for any reason they desire to get a prisoner punished, or if it is desirable in order to exculpate themselves from blame.

If this class of warders had to control only the habitual criminal, I do not think it would matter, they could not reduce *their* standard of morality, and they could scarcely do them an injustice.

If the Government adopt the recommendation of the Commission as to a classification of prisoners, let them, if they must retain the services of this class of men, confine them to the superintendence of the abandoned and the irreclaimable, and seek the services of a higher and better class of men to control those prisoners who are not dead to all sense of shame and decency, and who are amenable to good influences.

A case occurs to me which happened at Dartmoor last winter. It came under my own observation, for I knew both prisoner and officer, and it happened while I was at work close to the scene of it. A prisoner, Jones,—nicknamed "Parson Jones,"—had fallen out from his party to see the doctor. The assistant-warder, as was his duty, searched Parson Jones's clothes, and found no prohibited articles in them. Shortly after, the infirmary-warder came in, and gave Jones's clothes another search, not knowing that his subaltern had done so. He was smarter than the assistant-warder, and found some brass weights belonging to the infirmary scales in the prisoner's pocket.

Now, to have stolen these was of course a very serious offence, and would certainly subject the prisoner to three days' bread-and-water, a month's penal class diet, loss of three months' remission, which is tantamount to three months' longer imprisonment, and the loss of all his class privileges, tea, letter-writing, &c. Fortunately for the prisoner, and unfortunately for the corrupt warder, the latter was seen by another officer to deposit these weights in the prisoner's pocket. The prisoner was able to prove that the officer had more than once shown animosity towards him, and he of course committed this dastardly act to get the man unjustly punished.

Now, although this man was removed from his post in the infirmary for a few months, he has since been reinstated in his old position. I venture to suggest that his retention in the service is not calculated to inspire in the minds of prisoners — or such of them as have minds — a proper reverence and respect for the system of morality and justice under which they live.

The necessity for a more careful selection of prison-warders has been forced upon the attention of the Department since I commenced to pen these pages. A covey of convicts took flight from a hay-field at Dartmoor. The details of the affair were specially interesting to me, because in the summer of 1878 I was myself a haymaker in the field from which the exodus took place. The gang of convicts employed there on this occasion was called "thirty-four" party, and were in charge of two assistant-warders and a "civil guard," all of whom were armed with loaded rifles, and all of whom are well-known to me.

The senior, who had command of the party, is a Devonian peasant, who entered the British army at a time when recruits were not culled from that section of the community which our Yankee friends would call "high-toned."

He is a free-and-easy, baccy-and-beer-loving old pensioner, who, if he can push through his duties without a fine and get behind his pipe at the "Spotted Dog" in Princetown, is happier than the Queen he serves.

He has the character amongst convicts of being a "square man" and "as right as a trivet"; in other words, the discipline in his regiment is so. If a convict—an ordinary convict—speaks of an officer as a good fellow, he means that he is a man who does not do his duty, and will allow prisoners to evade labour and break rules with impunity. This officer is, I admit, a good-natured fellow; after dinner he is especially good-natured, and, like many another old soldier, he can lean upon his musket and take "forty winks." He had the misfortune to have as his assistant on the day in question a very young officer who was *not* an "old soldier" in any sense of the words, and who not long ago was a wheelwright in a Devonshire village. He is a well-intentioned, good-natured young countryman, but it is doing him no injustice to say that he is as green as was the grass which the men he should have controlled had been vainly trying to make into hay, and which I am credibly informed was so bad in quality that it will be spurned by every intelligent and well-bred horse.

The civil guard on the occasion I allude to was not one of those officious persons who always want to know what is going on. He was content to chew his quid and let his eye wander over the hills towards the paternal hut in dear old Tavistock, and was probably at the moment of the escapade contrasting his own distinguished position as "an officer in her Majesty's service," in receipt of an income of twenty-three shillings per week, with that of his dear old plodding brother, who was working ten times as hard for half the money away over the moor.

A day or two ago I received a letter from a prisoner of education, whom I can testify to be one of the few convicts who may be expected to seek readmission to the ranks of the virtuous when he is released. His letter, of course, came to me by the "Underground Railroad." It will be seen that he was attached to "thirty-four party" at the time of the flight :—

"DARTMOOR, 8*th September*, 1879.

"DEAR ——,

* * * * *

"I suppose there has been quite a 'flare-up' in the London newspapers about the recent escapade. As you will recollect, I am attached to "thirty-four party," so that I saw all the fun. The escape had been planned during the day. I was not invited to join in it because it was known in the party that I had but a few months to serve, and it would have been sheer madness to risk three months' further detention for any such 'wild-goose chase.'

"It was, indeed, a wild-goose chase. I said it was planned. There was, in fact, no plan; it was talked about, but the only agreement was that each man was to take a different route so as to divide the pursuing hounds. One of the runaways, a man named Morgan, was looked up to by the rest as an authority. He had last year escaped from the custody of an officer familiarly known as 'Billy Rowe.' On that occasion he chose a foggy day, and actually eluded his pursuers for three or four days, and was finally captured by a baker in the neighbourhood of Plymouth. I may mention, incidentally, that on that occasion a defect of vision and the fog combined, caused warder 'Billy Rowe' to mistake a brother officer for the runaway, and to pepper Her Majesty's uniform with shot.

"Convict Morgan assured his comrades that his capture was all because he wandered to the precincts of a great city, and that had he kept to the open country, hiding by day and travelling by night, he could have reached 'New Babylon' and been lost in the mazes of Whitechapel.

"The vision of convicts, artful and cunning as the majority of them are, seems to be obfuscated when the very possibility of regaining liberty is danced before their eyes. I pointed out to them that the difficulties were insuperable, that it was a perfectly clear night, and that almost every object upon the moor for twenty miles was visible. I also reminded them that within a circle of five miles there was a perfect cordon of labourers' huts, and that the only possible and remote chance which any of the denizens of these huts had of becoming the possessor of a five-pound note was in catching a convict.

"I suggested to them that Captain Harris, the Governor, and Captain Johnson, the Deputy-Governor, had swift horses, and were probably dead-shots with the rifle. I told them that a man in a convict's dress who was known to be a thief or a ruffian could not expect assistance or aid even if he got into the hands of those who would not be tempted by a reward.

"They were not to be balked in their scheme, they meant to have a try for it, and they did; a very foolish and sorry try it was. I quite agree with a remark which I heard principal warder Rundle make the next morning, that if the officers in charge had been at all awake to their duty no such escapade would have been possible. We had stacked our rakes and forks, so that we were entirely unarmed, and three officers armed with loaded rifles were in charge of us. We were unwisely allowed to go alone to the hedge, which was at a considerable distance, to fetch our clothes.

"'Now is our chance!' said Morgan, and over the hedge went the conspirators. As I was one who remained behind I could take stock of the officers in charge. They were supposed to be 'on guard.' I must say I never saw men so completely taken 'off their guard.' They looked very like the historical 'stuck' animal, the brothers and sisters of which they are far better qualified to take charge of than of convicts.

Had the capture depended upon these officers, or even of their brother warders, the convicts might to-day be starving in some ditch across these barren moors, instead of revelling as they are at this moment in a pint of good thick shin-of-beef-soup, a pound of potatoes, and six ounces of bread, at the expense of British taxpayers.

"But of their escape there was no fear. Thirty or forty Devonshire labourers had heard the alarm-whistle and the signal gun. They were soon joined by others, and in strong parties started in pursuit. They are wise in their generation, these Devon peasants, and not ambitious of making a name for themselves by the exhibition of individual prowess. They hunted in gangs, thinking it far wiser not to risk single-handed an encounter with desperadoes. I think I may safely say that for the reward for each capture there will be at least half-a-dozen claimants. Let no man for the future say that good never comes out of evil. A score or more of poor Devonians have anticipated Michaelmas and become the joyful possessors of a whole golden sovereign; perhaps some poor slipshod daughter will get a new pair of boots, and then she will dream that the golden age has come, and that there have been two harvests in one year.

"We, cowards, who did not desert the flag, were marched back to the prison under guard. We found on our way back, and on arriving at the prison, that the soul of each official was 'in arms, and eager for the fray.' On the road we met an excited, pale-faced youth, who, I believe, is a compounder of drugs in the medical department. He was flourishing a double-barrel shotgun in a most alarming manner, and was exclaiming, perhaps under the influence of some potent drug, 'Which way have they gone? Who will I shoot?' He has been the butt of a good many jokes since; for it was discovered when the time came to shoot that he had left his ammunition-pouch at his quarters. I have great hopes of obtaining from a kind-hearted official, who is handy with his pencil and his camera, a sketch or two in connection with this 'flight of convicts,' which will amuse the public if published.

"Of course, you know that the runaways were all caught. Last Friday Director Morrish came down to Dartmoor redolent with the odour of Whitehall, and armed in all the majesty of a supreme Judge. In accordance with his sentence five of the men received 'two dozen' each with the 'cat,' and the other three, whom the doctors would not pass for the 'cat,' were 'birched.'

" Speaking of the 'cat,' I hear that the public mind has been very much exercised lately on the subject of the 'cat'; and, so far as our gallant soldiers and sailors are concerned, I should be glad to see its use dispensed with. Allow me, at the same time, to assure you that to abolish its use in the convict service would be a blunder. I think you will agree with me that it is the only thing that prevents the 'old lags' from committing many acts of violence. No sentence of penal servitude frightens them. Both you and I have heard them say they can 'do it on their heads.' They are, however, all arrant cowards, and they stand in mortal dread of the 'cat.' I cannot think, old friend, that there can be any cruelty in administering moderate doses of it to some of the brutes you and I are acquainted with here, especially when we remember that they live by systematic plunder when free. I feel very certain that nothing but the fear of the 'cat' prevents them from setting the authorities at defiance when they are in prison.

"I saw the runaways this morning in their yellow dresses; they are breaking stones, which I hope will be used to mend the road between here and the railway-station before I go home, for I am told it is in a horrible state.

"This morning the governor received from Parliament-street the decision of the directors as to the punishment of the officers who were in charge of the runaways. They are each fined 10s., and reduced to probation-class for three months, so that their pay will be decreased for that period; and our old friend ——— will have to curtail the number of his visits to the 'Spotted Dog.'

"I must say good-bye, old fellow, and seal up my despatch; for I expect the postman every minute.—Believe me your obliged friend,

"———."

I have spoken incidentally of prison punishments—I mean penalties inflicted for a breach of prison discipline—and I have said that these fall the most heavily on the unsophisticated. I will here add that these punishments are constantly inflicted for offences which are certainly not crimes, and that therefore some strict rules ought to control governors, who at present exercise unrestrained power.

A man who has been deprived of all knowledge of what has been going on in the world for half-a-dozen years picks up a piece of an old newspaper a few inches square which has been blown on to the works at Portland from the neighbouring barracks. Not being an old gaol-bird, with his eyes and ears everywhere, he is detected in the act of reading it, taken before the governor, and sentenced to three days' bread-and-water diet in a punishment-cell, deprived of a portion of his clothing and all his bedding, reduced to an inferior class for three months, which modifies his diet and deprives him of the privilege of communicating with, or being visited by, his relatives, and he is fined a number of marks, the effect of which is to keep him a fortnight longer in prison.

It is sometimes an infraction of prison rules to do things which are absolutely a necessity, and which I have yet seen frequently punished by deprivation of food and loss of marks. It is, of course, at the option of warders to report men for such offences, or not to report them. An officer having charge of a ward, and who has in any of his cells a prisoner who is obnoxious to him, can always make an occasion to get rid of him, and many are unscrupulous enough to exercise their "little brief authority."

When a prisoner is reported and punished, he is removed to what are called the "separate cells," and when his two or three days of punishment have expired the cell he formerly occupied has found a new tenant, and he probably goes to another ward, and often to quite a different part of the prison. It is quite common, therefore, for unprincipled officers to make reports against prisoners whom they consider troublesome. I have heard more than one officer promise a prisoner that he would "get rid of him."

One Sunday morning, I think it was in 1875, but as diaries are not allowed in convict prisons I cannot fix the exact date, an event occurred in what is called E hall, at Portland, which should have been a stern rebuke to the class of officers who misuse the power with which they are invested. A very young man named Wills, of former respectability and of some education and intelligence, was the occupant of a cell upon the top landing of the hall. He had been suffering for several weeks from diarrhœa, and had been on more than one occasion subjected to punishment for committing an act which it was quite impossible for him to avoid.

On this Sunday morning he repeated the so-called offence under necessity, and his warder notified him that on Monday morning he should report him to the governor. Poor young Wills had nearly completed his sentence; he had but a few weeks to serve; his anxious and heart-broken mother was making preparation to welcome home her prodigal son; he was counting the days which stood between him and freedom; his prison spoon had served him for a "wooden calendar," and he had just scored off with childish glee " the daily notch."

To be taken before the governor on Monday morning was to be condemned to at least another week of imprisonment. The threat was too horrible to the poor boy; he was in exceedingly delicate health,—consumption had wasted his frame; he had told me that the highest of his hopes for this world was that he might be restored to freedom, in order to die in his mother's arms. Another week! The thought was too dreadful for a mind weakened by a combination of disease, dissipation, and remorse. He could be patient no longer under "hope deferred." He made one spring over the balustrade, and his body lay upon the flags below; the leap was as from the top of a four-story house, and it was fatal. He was carried to the infirmary, and, when the prison-bell tolled for vespers, he had gone to his everlasting rest.

I recollect this young Wills very well some seven years ago. He was at that time a clerk in the office of a Covent Garden hotel, which was once the resort of the "famous" who desired to beguile the witching hour, but is now, I believe, a favourite rendezvous of a very different class. The boy was often thrown into the society of sporting men; he became "horsey," and "made a book." I have just spoken the epilogue to his drama of life.

I may tell of another instance of the exercise of arbitrary power on the part of warders which more nearly affected myself, and which lengthened the time of my incarceration by some six weeks. I had a great desire to improve the hours which I had to spend in my cell, and when I could obtain a volume which contained selections from the works of the great poets I was accustomed to memorize them.

To copy them would, of course, greatly facilitate my object, but prison regulations forbid both pencil and writing-paper. As "love"—akin in this respect to burglars—"laughs at locksmiths," so prisoners laugh at prohibitions of this sort. Brown wrapping-paper, which was served out for necessary purposes, I converted into tablets, and a small piece of common plumber's lead which I had picked up upon the works did duty for a

L

pencil. I scribbled away for many weeks, and, with the aid of these accessories, drummed many thousands of lines from Shakspeare and Milton, and Wordsworth and Shelley, and dear little Keats, into my memory. A very good fellow had charge of the landing on which my cell was situated; he had watched "my little game," and having satisfied himself that, although a breach of prison-rules, it was yet harmless, he had allowed me to pursue "the even tenor of my way."

One morning I missed his friendly face. He had gone "on leave" for a week. His place was supplied by a plausible, but cadaverous-looking "screw," who had been constantly reported and fined by the governor for derelictions of duty. It was no doubt a very important thing for him to distinguish himself, if possible; but I must say that I was exceedingly sorry to be the stepping-stone on his way back to official favour. I cannot tell whether or no some prisoner gave him "the tip," but in my absence at chapel he made a raid on my cell, and in one of the folds of my hammock discovered the implements which were aiding my acquirements in literature.

It was a grand foray for him. He established his reputation for 'cuteness, and his former little peccadilloes were condoned. For me the result was not so cheerful. Governor Clifton came to the conclusion that I was trying to acquire knowledge in a dangerous way, and thought it wise to cool my courage and reduce my energies by a little enforced abstinence. I was sentenced to three days upon bread-and-water, to be succeeded by fourteen days of penal-class diet, the loss of all my class privileges, letter-writing, tea, &c. &c., and to be deprived of the use of all books for three months; and, worst of all, I was fined as many marks as would add six weeks to the time of my imprisonment.

A good warder, who really would have reported any prisoner guilty of a wrong act, had winked at my harmless infraction of a hard-and-fast rule. An incompetent officer, who was at the time in bad odour, and who had himself broken half the rules of the service, was able to win laurels by making me his victim. I regret to say that this was not the only instance in my own prison history of the exercise of dangerous power on the part of warders for petty and selfish motives.

During the term of my imprisonment I was never reported for the use of bad language, or for laziness, or for talking with other prisoners, or for the possession of tobacco, or for any of the other crimes for which prisoners are very properly punished; but I was, nevertheless, detained in prison nearly seven months longer than I ought to have been, in order to atone for so-called offences, the morality of which could not be condemned by the Archbishop of Canterbury himself.

I saw several instances of punishment at Dartmoor which I certainly thought most barbarous. Men employed in the tailors' or shoemakers' shops have no great appetite for their food, whilst others who are at out-door work upon the moor are ravenous. The former would out of sheer kindness frequently throw half-a-pound of their bread to the hungry ones, but if caught doing so by the officer on duty, they are taken before the governor, and sentenced to undergo the punishment I have described in connection with the newspaper.

A man scarcely able to read or write wishes to send a letter to his anxious wife at home; he gets his more educated neighbour to compose a letter for him on his slate, which he can afterwards transcribe. They are detected, and both sentenced to the "three days" with the etceteras. On the day for distributing the library books an educated prisoner will perhaps get some childish tale, and his next-door neighbour, who cannot read will get Milton's immortal epic; an exchange is made, the *crime* is discovered, and the bread-and-water with their concomitants follow. These things occur every day, and I respectfully suggest that their influence is to harden and barbarize the prisoner, and to destroy all feelings of reverence for the authorities.

When the question of prison punishments came up in the House of Commons in the session of 1879 Mr. Cross succeeded in mystifying his assailants, who of course had no practical experience of the working of the system. He told them that in the *county prisons* he had put it out of the power of governors to inflict bread-and-water diet for a longer period than twenty-four hours, that is, twenty-four hours at a time, but even under this regulation a man may be sentenced to four days' bread-and-water out of seven, there being one day intervening between each punishment. But let it be understood that in *convict* prisons no such restriction exists. There, a man may still be sentenced to *three* days' bread-and-water on the Saturday. On the Tuesday he would come off punishment, and get a day's second-class diet, but could be reported again on that day, and sentenced to three days more, which would commence on the Wednesday; he would then come off punishment on Saturday, and after getting one day's second-class diet, could be sentenced to *another* three days.

I have known many prisoners to do twenty-one days out of a month upon bread-and-water, and in every case the victim was a man unaccustomed to prison discipline, who had been made a mark by some prison-warder anxious for promotion, and who had goaded the poor fellow into using violent and threatening language. The old thieves, as I have said, never fall into these traps, and, on account of the combination existing amongst them, they are let alone by nine out of ten of the officers. When one of these attempts to do his duty with the professional thieves he gets murdered, or very nearly so, as in the case of poor Luscombe; and so it will be whilst the present system of association affords the opportunity for conspiracy.

A few months ago a poor mulatto youth was transferred to Dartmoor prison from Portsmouth. He had there got into trouble, first over a piece of tobacco not bigger than a sixpence. An officer made a "mark" of him, seeing that he was a green hand, and got him punished over and over again. At last he carried his animosity too far. The fellow's black blood was roused, and he struck his enemy. He was flogged, and sent in chains to Dartmoor. There the whole brood of officers, or "screws," as the "lags" call them, got down upon him; he was reported time after time, and during the early part of this year he had existed for *fifty days* out of three months upon bread-and-water, and in the middle of March I left him in the hospital in a very precarious state, as the result of his punishment.

There are men punished every day at all the stations for the possession of *tobacco*. It is considered by the governors and directors (next to the striking of an officer) as the most flagrant breach of prison discipline, and yet every particle of tobacco which finds its way to a prisoner *must* do so through the hands of warders, or other Government servants. It will be seen how dangerous a power is thus put into the hands of a band of men, for the most part illiterate and unprincipled. If an officer, as is often the case, and of which the infirmary warder to whom I have referred, is an example, takes a dislike to a well-conducted novice in crime, who avoids association alike with prisoners and officers, he may have no real ground of complaint against him, but he has only to drop a quarter of an inch of tobacco in the man's cell, and instruct another officer to find it, and the prisoner is sure of a most severe punishment. I have *known* this to be practised upon a man who never used tobacco in his life, and who certainly never willingly had any in his possession.

There is a warder still in the service, and on duty at Dartmoor, who being very desirous to get a man into trouble, one morning, when searching him on parade, put his hand into the jacket pocket, produced a *mite* of tobacco, exclaiming, "I thought I smelt it." I, and several other prisoners, knowing the accused and the *accuser*, were thoroughly satisfied that the tobacco was between the fingers before the hand went into the pocket; but the prisoner was reported, he was sentenced to three days' bread-and-water; he then got three days more for making a false accusation against the officer, and a further three days for impertinence to the governor. He was then put into close confinement for twenty-one days upon penal-class diet, which is about half-way between bread-and-water and full diet; he was not allowed to write to, or hear from, his wife and children for nine months, and he was sentenced to lose a number of marks which he had earned by industry and good conduct, such loss meaning a detention in prison for three additional months. This man had never been in prison before, and of this offence I am *certain* he was not guilty.

I admit that a governor cannot take a prisoner's evidence against an officer's, but I submit that so dangerous a power should not be placed in the hands of such a class as fill the office of prison-warders.

Surely it is the duty of governors and directors to make some very stringent regulations which shall prevent officers bringing tobacco into convict prisons, or else abstain from visiting the possession of it by prisoners with such severe punishment. A man accustomed to the use of tobacco would need have some moral courage to refuse it when offered him, and if, as is often the case, it is put into his possession against his will, and he is then punished, he naturally ceases to have any respect for the law or its administrators. Of course I know many prisoners are only too ready to obtain tobacco in *any* way. I knew twenty or thirty prisoners at Portland, and as many at Dartmoor, who were, through their relatives, paying officers at the rate of thirty shillings per pound for tobacco. These were old thieves, who knew the ropes and were too cunning to be caught; but the existence of the traffic does not speak very highly for the *morale* of the officers employed or for the sharpness of their superiors.

Old gaol-birds are not often caught in this tobacco business, they are too wary and too lynx-eyed; and, besides that, I am sorry to say they stand on too friendly a footing with the warders who have charge of them, and whose duty it is to report them. A large proportion of the warders seem to deal with men who have done two or three laggings as old and familiar friends, instead of trying, as they should do, to make the prison a very hot place for them.

Before leaving this part of the question, I will just say that while I hold that convicts are not made to work half hard enough, and that there is very little fault to be found with the diet, I think there are many abuses connected with the infliction of prison punishments which require to be remedied. Some governors seem to have a mania for inflicting the bread-and-water punishment, and they do this for so-called offences which are certainly not crimes.

Surely, men who are appointed to the office of governor, and who are entrusted with so much dangerous power, should be carefully selected, and should know how to temper not only mercy, but reason with justice. Of course the governors are not all alike. The present estimable and admirable governor of Millbank Prison inflicts less punishments in a year than others do in a month with the same number of men. When he is absent for a week's leave, the number of punishments is at once increased by his subaltern, and certainly without any improvement in the good order and discipline of the prison.

On reading this description of "prison punishment," some one will exclaim, "Where are the directors of the convict department, whose duty it is to visit prisons, and hear the complaints of prisoners?" Six years in penal servitude have convinced me that the ten thousand pounds appropriated to this department is a fraud upon the taxpayers. There are ten convict prisons.

I am sure that one thoroughly competent and conscientious man might visit all these prisons, inspect the food supplied and all the internal arrangements, hear the appeals and complaints of prisoners, remedy many abuses, and save many thousands a year to the public.

The four or five ornamental gentlemen for whom it has been necessary to find a billet, and who now fill the office of directors, are supposed to visit each prison once a month; in reality, they manage so as to make about eleven visits in a year. No visiting director has more than two country prisons to attend to. The day before he makes his visit a telegram informs the governor of his advent, the yards are swept up, the governor puts on his "Lincoln & Bennett" or "Christy," the chief warder dons his belt and sword! the old soldiers amongst the warders put on all their medals, the soup in one of the coppers is made a little thicker than usual, and the great man arrives. He walks round the prison with the governor.

As when the governor goes his rounds, so with the director, the principal warders give the office to the warders, and the warders telegraph to the assistant-warders that the director approaches; he is assured that everything is right. He sees what it is intended he should see, and nothing more. Much in the same way that an audience at a theatre witnesses a drama; he sees and knows nothing about the wires, and the ropes, and the traps, and the wings; he sees only what is made visible by the footlights.

The delusion over, he proceeds to the judgment-room to listen to the complaints of prisoners, and to hear charges against officers and prisoners which are of a serious nature, and which have been reserved for his judgment. In the six years of my experience I knew of many acts committed by governors which could scarcely be regarded as just, but never one single instance of the injustice being rectified by the director. Every prisoner who goes before the director with a complaint is, to use a prison phrase, "choked off." The director is merely ornamental. He makes a formal visit of two or three hours' duration eleven times a year, in order to father everything that the governor has done.

> In fair round belly, with good capon lined,
> With eyes severe, and beard of formal cut,
> Full of wise saws and modern instances,
> He plays his part.

He nods, he eats eleven luncheons at the expense of the governor or the country,—I know not which,—praises the claret, nods again, and has then earned his thousand pounds. This will continue until men are selected for different reasons and in a different way.

The gentleman who is the visiting director of two of the most important convict prisons,—Portland and Dartmoor,—has held office either as governor or director for many years. He was entrusted with the important duties appertaining to these offices, shortly after a madman named Oxford had made an attack upon the Queen. I believe that he effected the arrest of the culprit, and so entitled himself to some reward; but I submit that this service should not have been considered a sufficient qualification for the important duties which he has been called upon to fulfil during the last thirty years or more.

CHAPTER VII.

REFORMATORY AND SANATORY.

I THINK it is not generally known, and the matter seems to have altogether escaped the notice of the Commission which has recently reported, that about one-third of the cells at Portland, more than one-half of the cells at Dartmoor, and corresponding numbers at other country stations, are what the prisoners not unreasonably call "dark cells"; they have no direct light; all that they have is borrowed from the corridor or hall into which they open.

In the evening, even in the summer-time, it is quite impossible to read in them, and it is only with the greatest difficulty that a man with good eyes can see to read at noon; the only time, therefore, which a prisoner occupying these cells has for reading is in the winter, and by gaslight.

This, however, is not the greatest evil connected with them. A very large proportion of the prisoners belong to that class who "love darkness rather than light, because their deeds are evil," and these dark cells are a cover for all sorts of immorality and indecency, about which I cannot be more communicative. Light and air are moral as well as physical necessaries.

Then the cells of which I speak are exceedingly small, and only divided from each other by a thin sheet of corrugated iron; a man with good ears can listen to his neighbour's yarns even without the aid of a "chat-hole." It is the custom, however, for prisoners to bore a small hole through the partition, near to the ground, through which the chat takes place. The one prisoner lies down on the ground and talks and listens, with his mouth or ear to the chat-hole; his neighbour sits at the window, which opens on to the landing along which the officer in charge walks. If he approaches, a knock from the watcher causes the chat to be suspended until he has passed, when it commences again.

The separate system, while these cells are tolerated, is altogether a farce. If two old thieves are next door to each other, the filthy conversation which takes place may be imagined. All sorts of villanies and conspiracies are concocted in these dark cells, and if the man on either side of the "chatters" happens to be a novice in crime, he has the opportunity of taking lessons in rascality. If he be a man of any decency his attention is diverted from his book; if he happen to have a light and could otherwise read it.

These thieves, too, are the most persistent talkers that can possibly be imagined; they are constitutionally law-breakers, and the fact that talking is prohibited is with them a sufficient reason for talking without ceasing, and *such* talk!

I had the misfortune to have one of the vagabonds next me at Portland. He was not only a moral but a physical nuisance; the effluvium which was exhaled from his body, and which was, I presume, the result of neglected disease, found its way through the chinks of my cell and disgusted me; while the emanations of his mouth were filthy beyond description, and would have created a moral pestilence anywhere.

I recollect a little of the family history which

this fellow repeated to me, and which is very characteristic of the estimation in which virtue and purity are regarded by all his class. He said that he had heard through "a pal of his who had been recently 'lagged,' that his old woman was living with another bloke." His great anxiety seemed to be to find out if she would be willing to come back to him on his discharge. He said she was a valuable old "———" to him, for she was cook at a restaurant in the City, and she always brought home enough "junk" and "toke" to fill his carcase, and he had all his thievings for liquor. He also regaled me, very much against my will, with descriptions of his marauding expeditions. I certainly had every opportunity to learn the trade of a sneak-thief.

At another time I had a neighbour who had heard from somebody that I had some respectable connections. The scoundrel seriously proposed that, after we were both released, I should "put him up" to getting anything I saw in places to which I had the *entrée*. He was willing to take all the risk, and I was to go halves in the plunder,

Now, only think, there are hundreds of youths and young men convicted every year for the first time; many men of all ages, who have some human feelings, which even ignorance and drink and sin have not eliminated; men who have a common nature which could be impressed, minds which could be instructed, sympathies which could be drawn back to virtue, and souls which might be purified and restored.

The Government takes each of these unfortunates and puts him into a dark cell, where his only possible occupation is to talk to a professional villain, and be by him initiated into the mysteries and advantages of a dishonest life. A poor wretched agricultural labourer is made the near neighbour, night and day, of a scoundrel who qualifies him and renders him capable of committing a burglary at the residence of his old employer within a week after his discharge from prison.

He goes to the convict prison for the perpetration of perhaps one petty offence, committed under the influence of drink or poverty, and, thanks to a paternal Government, he leaves prison thoroughly qualified to execute every hideous crime in the calendar. At first many of these young criminals are so ignorant that, to save their lives, they could not *spell* house or watch, and in the *spelling* they are no better off when they leave than when they enter; but the law has given them some very able tutors who have taught them how to break into the one and to snatch the other.

Drink leads nine-tenths of prisoners into crime: no sane man doubts that; but then the law takes these amateurs, and throws them into the arms of professionals, in these dark and easily-communicating cells; and unless they have some really good principles which whisky has not destroyed, and a large share of moral courage, they are rapidly imbued with principles which laugh at all moral restraints.

I *repeat*, because I think the evil cannot be over-estimated, there are hundreds and hundreds of men now in the convict prisons who occupy every moment which they spend in their cell, which is not devoted to sleep, in vicious and filthy conversations with their next neighbour, and in watching and perfecting conspiracies against life and property. Old and hardened criminals teach each other new dodges, and become more proficient in crime; and novices are by these old and hardened criminals transformed into adepts.

I have already said something about the Medical Department of the Convict Service. I am quite within the truth when I say that the doctors are the hardest-worked and the worst-paid of prison officials. They have great responsibilities, and if they happen to make a mistake they are amenable to all sorts of penalties. I think they deserve sympathy and consideration at the hands of the public, and with few exceptions they are entitled to the full confidence of the community. There may be one here and there who would be better in health, and of more service to the State, if he preferred milk to brandy, but such cases are exceptional ones, and would not exist if there were a head to the system who was responsible to Parliament and who would personally investigate what goes on.

The unsophisticated would scarcely believe how arduous and difficult are the duties of a medical officer in a convict prison. He has to measure his shrewdness and judgment against the deceit and the cunning of the most villanously artful and deceitful body of men in the world.

The first object of every professional thief and habitual criminal after his conviction is to do something to himself, or to invent some ingenious lie, by which he can "fetch the farm," which is thieves' language for obtaining admission to the infirmary. A prisoner there gets a good bed and the close association of forty other thieves in a large warm dormitory. He gets nice food, and he gets what every thief in England adores above everything else except drink: I mean entire laziness. He can lie on his back, eat, talk filth to his neighbour, and plot future villany. The infirmary is the convicted thief's paradise, and he leaves no stone unturned to get into it.

When one old "lag" is successful in any invention which gains him admission, he communicates with his pal, and unless a doctor is very wide awake he may be humbugged into the idea that some particular malady has been engendered in the prison by bad water or food, or gas, whereas the infection has only emanated from diseased and villanous imaginations. The prisoners are continually comparing notes with each other as to the best means of "besting the croker."

When I was discharged from the infirmary and returned to the prison it was at dinner-time. I was located in a vacant cell, and could hear my neighbour eating his dinner. The officer locked me in and went away, but had not got many yards along the corridor when I heard a knock, succeeded by a voice.

"Did you come from the 'farm,' mate?"

"Yes."

"Did you get full diet?"

"Yes."

"Any extras?"

"Yes."

"Any beer?"

"No."

"Why not?"

"Because I preferred milk."

"Look here, old chum. I'll give you a 'wing

of snout' (that is, a taste of tobacco) if you'll tell me how you worked it. What did you complain of when the croker took you in?"

"Nothing!"

"Who was it? Askham?"

"No. Bernard."

"And he took you in for nothing?"

"He examined me, and put me to bed."

This was not satisfactory to my "co-mate and brother in exile." I don't think he believed me, and I did not get the "wing of snout." The next day when I went out upon the works, I was beset by similar inquiries, and got plenty of curses for not being more communicative.

All sorts of dodges are resorted to. Bidwell is not the only one who feigns paralysis; many poison their flesh by inserting in it copper-wire or worsted; others swallow ground glass, eat poisonous insects, swallow soap and soda, or slightly maim and disable themselves. Anything by which they can secure a skulk, and escape from what Mr. Carlyle has wisely called the "sacredness of work." The most earnest prayer of the professional thief might be thus translated:

"From the sacredness of work, and from all other sacredness, good Lord deliver me."

When the thief once gets his foot into the infirmary, his two anxieties are how to stop there, and how to obtain " extras," especially beer. He compares notes with some other rascal, and tries a fresh hoax every day upon the doctor. If the doctor were to believe what he is told by professional thieves, one-half of their whole number would be constantly in the infirmary; and if he believed the stories of those whom he does admit, he would never get rid of them until the day of their discharge, for, according to their own account, they get worse every day. The commonest answer by an habitual criminal to the doctor's morning inquiry, is, " I don't feel near as well as I did yesterday, doctor. I feel so weak and so faint. I think I should get strong if you'd give me some porter"!! And half of them are all the time thoroughly well, thoroughly strong, and lie on their lazy backs hour after hour inventing fresh hoaxes.

At Portland and Dartmoor, and I believe at all other provincial stations, the casual sick are seen by the doctor in the dinner-hour. This is an evil in many ways, and the discontinuance of the practice has been recommended in the Report of the recent Commission. To give prisoners medicine with their dinner is ridiculous, and in many cases useless; and it *is* given literally *with* the dinner. I recollect distinctly that almost every day when the cells were being unlocked for the men whose names were down for the doctor, I had about half-finished my dinner, and if I were really unwell and required a dose of medicine, my only opportunity of taking it was either to go without my dinner altogether, or take rhubarb or castor-oil as a sort of sandwich between beef and bread.

But let it be understood that this arrangement is not under the control of the doctor, it is made by the governor for the convenience of himself and his subalterns. There is no good reason why the medicine should not be dispensed in the early morning as soon as prisoners rise, and half-an-hour before breakfast. I know that on the last day of July an order was issued directing a change in this respect, but I also know, that a week after that date no change had been made at Dartmoor, so I presume the authorities there are creating difficulties.

I would also suggest that if the doctor, accompanied by his dispenser, went to the cells of those men who had applied to see him in the same way that he does at Pentonville Prison, all opportunity for trafficking and assignations by prisoners at the doctor's hour would be avoided, and the doctor would be saved quite a number of bogus applications, for, as I have already intimated, a large number of prisoners only apply to see the doctor in order to keep an appointment with a " chum."

I may mention here that the disgusting custom of stripping a lot of prisoners naked in the presence and sight of each other for the purpose of searching is still continued at Dartmoor. Clause 25 of the Commissioners' Report says that it has been discontinued since the Commission commenced its sittings. This is not so. At the beginning of the month of August, 1879, I am informed that a whole party of twenty or thirty men were taken into the hall of the separate cells, and stripped in the presence of each other. It was done almost every day while I was at that station, and I have good authority for saying that the disgusting and immoral practice still continues. It is certainly not calculated to raise the standard of decency amongst the criminal class.

I have taken it for granted in all that I have said that the State has duties beyond the mere punishment of crime. Millions are spent annually for that purpose. Millions are stolen annually by the criminal from the honest and industrious classes, and spent in those great receiving-houses of stolen money—the gin-palaces and the brothels. Now, is it possible to do anything towards the *prevention* of crime? If so, surely it is a duty incumbent on the State. I think it will be possible when a proper classification of prisoners has been made. The money now expended upon the educational department is altogether thrown away, absolutely squandered and wasted. I have watched the workings and effects of the school organization very carefully, and I am very sure that not one man in one thousand derives the slightest benefit from it.

I am not alone in this opinion. A Catholic

priest who has, I believe, been in the service since Catholic priests were first employed, told me only a few days ago that he had the very worst opinion of the influences of the present convict system upon the morals of the prisoners; that he had seen *no good effects whatever from the school teaching*, and that without great reform he was quite sure he never would.

Now, there are thousands of prisoners unable either to read or write their own names, and whose ignorance has been one of the great obstacles to their success in life; there are hundreds of agricultural labourers, who, although they are in prison, are not vicious by nature or inclination; and there are numbers of young boys who have landed in prison in absolute ignorance, and whose presence there is due to the fact that they have been allowed to grow up without any mental or moral training. These classes have now the opportunity of attending school for *one hour in a week* in the winter time, and for about *twenty minutes in a week* in summer time!

During these minutes the boy, the countryman,

the novice in crime, sit shoulder to shoulder with old and abandoned thieves. These old thieves have not the most remote intention to learn, even if they had the opportunity, but they attend school as an excuse to get out of their cells, and because they want a change of scene and company.

When prisoners are entitled to write letters to their friends they write them in the school-hour, so that I had frequent opportunities of seeing what went on. Disgusting conversations were indulged in, the prisoners keeping their eyes upon their books to avoid detection, but under pretence of mumbling their lessons aloud they were engaged in ribald chat with their neighbours, and many were making disgusting and licentious drawings on their slates, and showing them to their pals. Classification would remedy this evil, for it is only caused by the habitual-criminal element. The other classes would profit by instruction if they had any opportunity, at present they have no chance given them.

I will describe the educational arrangements at Dartmoor. They reflect precisely the state of things at Portland, and I presume at the other public-works prisons. There are five distinct prisons or halls. Once a week, in each hall, in summer for about twenty minutes and in winter for about one hour, the schoolmasters instruct, or pretend to instruct, such prisoners as can neither read nor write; no others are permitted to attend school. An utter ignorance of the history of England, or the geography of the globe, or of the simplest rules of arithmetic, are not considered sufficient reasons to warrant the interference of the schoolmaster.

The very little time allotted for educational purposes is half wasted even in this "once a week" system. When the bell rings for school and the classes have assembled the roll is called, then the schoolmasters (who do everything very leisurely) distribute the copybooks or the spelling-books; then they take another slow walk round with the pens, and by the time a dozen words of one syllable have been spelt, and often before a single line in the copybook has been filled, the bell rings again. The schoolmaster's work (?) is done, he walks—not leisurely round now, he wants to get home, or to the billiard-room in the village, and he is all in a bustle—"Now, then, hurry up with those books and pens! look sharp!" Then, away rush the "dominies," and the prisoners return to their cells about as wise as they left them. The only thing they have learned, is probably a fresh lesson in vice from their next neighbour, or the latest prison scandal and gossip.

I have certainly met with two or three men who, in spite of difficulties, have after three or four years acquired sufficient knowledge to scribble half-a-dozen ungrammatical lines to their friends; but these cases have been the result of prodigious effort, and are not the consequence of any interest which is taken in their work by the school-masters, who are paid very fair salaries, and whose great object seems to be to do as little as possible in return.

Now, why does not the Government utilize the services of this staff of expensive, and at present useless men? Taking the average of winter and summer, they are occupied for about forty-five minutes on five days of the week. The only other thing that the whole staff do between them is to leave a book once a week at each cell-door, and this is often too much for them; they frequently miss it. They take advantage of every possible excuse to avoid even their slight duties.

Last year the chaplain wished them to make a catalogue of the books in the library. I could have catalogued all the books they have there in six hours. It took these four or five indolent men three months to do it, and during that time it was impossible to get a readable book; and let it be borne in mind that such things as this only bear heavily on the novices in crime, like all the other regulations in the convict service. The old thieves don't care for books; you may as well give strawberries to pigs.

I complained to the chaplain several times while this cataloguing was going on and told him that a tenth of the library of the British Museum could have been catalogued in less time. He said, jokingly, that they were a lazy lot, and he feared he should have to get some of them "sacked," but they "hurried not."

I have shown in a former chapter that a great

portion of the labour done by convicts is wasted labour, and I am sure that none of it is remunerative. Now, would it not be wise to devote three afternoons in the week to the instruction of these ignorant men?

The Saturday, which is now a half-holiday, might be one of them, and, by a very little good management, the labour performed on the other two afternoons might be accomplished in the morning in addition to what is now done. If Mr. Cross will send for Captain Harris from Dartmoor, or Mr. Clifton from Portland, and put the question straight to them, I am quite sure that they will admit that it is possible to make arrangements by which nine hours in the week could be devoted to the education of the ignorant. The three hours on the Saturday at present so much misused by prisoners in their cells provides a third of the time, and by a very little extra energy the labour now accomplished on Tuesdays and Thursdays might be crowded into the mornings of those days.

Then these schoolmasters would have a little

occupation. At present they are getting fat from inaction, and their brains are getting mouldy from lack of exercise. They loll about with their fishing-rods, and ruminate upon the pension which they see looming in the future, but which they can scarcely delude themselves that they have honestly earned. To put it mildly, they are at present making no adequate return for the public money they receive.

I approach the religious question with some diffidence, because, while I am very anxious to expose the hypocrisy and deceit which are practised by the criminal class, I should indeed be sorry if it were supposed that I wished to cast any slur upon holy things. The programme of the religious department in a convict prison is made up of two services on the Sunday, with a sermon at each, and a monthly celebration of the Sacrament of the Lord's Supper. There is an early service every morning during the week for a few minutes. On Tuesday and Thursday a short address is given; on Wednesday and Friday the Litany is read; and on Monday and Saturday selections from the Morning Service of the Church. The services in the Roman Catholic chapels, are, I am told, of a similar character.

About the whole of these services there is a dead and hollow formality which always spoke to me of hideous and transparent hypocrisy. The prisoners are all glad to take part in these services, because they add a little variety to their life, and because they increased their opportunities for chat and association. Not one in a hundred goes into the chapel with any reverence for the God with whom he is supposed to hold communion. Not one in a hundred who join in the Confession of sin cares whether God hears them or not, but they speak loudly, and *do* care very much that the *chaplain* should hear them, and observe them, for upon his recommendation they may be able to obtain a more pleasant billet in the prison. At every opportunity during the service at least three-fourths of the prisoners utilize the responses and the prayers which are repeated after the clergyman for the purpose of conversation with one of their neighbours.

I have seen a man pulling a long face and

who, with his hands clasped and his eyes on the chaplain, instead of repeating the *Pater Noster*, was detailing to his chum the latest news from some thieves' quarter in London, which he had received through a man recently "lagged." It will be said that this sort of thing cannot be helped, but I think it is largely due to a want of earnestness on the part of the chaplains, and it is certainly due in a great measure to the too-frequent services, and their stereotyped character. Neither these men nor any other men, bond or free, in England, dream of going to church every day; why should convicts do so?

I sincerely believe that there are hundreds of men in convict prisons who are open to good influences. I think that an earnest practical appeal to them from the pulpit, showing them how utterly futile it is to expect real happiness in this world except from a life of virtue, or urging upon them the great truth that the most truly happy people in the world are those who subsist on the fruits of their labour, would really produce some good results. Now I am sorry to say that prison chaplains attach far more importance to doctrinal Christianity than to practical godliness. They are too constantly urging prisoners to believe that God sent them into the world under a curse; that they were created wicked by the constitution of their flesh, and wicked by eternal decree.

These abstruse disquisitions have no good effect upon the criminal class, nor upon unthinking men who do not yet belong to that class, and perhaps still less upon the few who *do* think. When thieves are told that they were born unable to keep the commandments, they rather naturally inquire why they are punished for breaking them, and so with other mysteries. When preached to about the atonement, they are assured that the sins of all who believe have been atoned for. They do not receive the doctrine *cum grano*, but literally; so they swear they believe, swallow the sacrament, think they are all right, and go on singing in chapel and cursing outside until the next sacrament-day. Now, would it not be better to discourse to these men on the great law of cause and effect; to try to show that honesty is indeed the best policy; and that peace and plenty and comfort can only follow purity and industry and sobriety?

Then such advice tendered to the mass might advantageously be followed up by personal appeals to such of the prisoners as are but new travellers on the "road to ruin." I do not speak of the old and incorrigible thieves, but outside of this class I am sure there are many to whom a little advice — not given as from a gaoler to a prisoner, but as from a large-hearted Christian man to an erring brother — would be thankfully welcomed.

I am sorry to say that during my long experience in two convict prisons I never knew a chaplain voluntarily to enter a prisoner's cell and have a little rational talk with him about the good policy of honesty and truth. I am sure that not one of them ever came in this way to me. I never heard of one going to any other prisoner. If I made an application to see a chaplain about a book or a letter, he generally gave me the impression that he made the note in his book without having the slightest interest in me or my reformation, and simply because it was a part of the routine which ensured him his salary. If a chaplain does call upon a prisoner it is to urge his attendance upon the Sacrament of the Lord's Supper.

I really think it would be wise on the part of the Government to prohibit this service altogether in convict prisons. Nothing in my prison-life disgusted me so much as the infamous use which is made of this ordinance of the Church. A large proportion of the vilest and filthiest scoundrels whom I met with, both at Portland and Dartmoor, were not only members of the church choir, and the loudest in their responses at church, but "regular communicants" of the Lord's Supper.

At Portland, and I presume at other stations, the chaplains have found it necessary to keep a tight hold upon the goblets while administering the wine. To trust them in the hands of the communicants would be to greatly increase the amount of the prison-wine account.

If the numbers who attend this service were a good test of the amount of real good achieved by the chaplains, they would surely deserve great credit. There are a legion of applicants for the bread and wine on the first Sunday of each month. The prisoners, rightly or wrongly, have got the idea that if they want an easy billet in the prison work—a job in the cook-house or bake-house, or a nurseship in the infirmary— their game is to pull a long face at chapel, and take the Sacrament regularly. The most unmitigated villains unhung would reverently turn to the east, and loudly mouth out the damnatory clauses of the Athanasian Creed, and I am bound to say that they made it pay. Reports, no doubt went up to the Home Secretary of the great amount of good accomplished; I must say that I fear it was nine-tenths humbug. The general result of the present system is to foster and perpetuate hypocrisy. The present leader of the choir in the Protestant chapel at Dartmoor, and one of the most devout prisoners (at church) is doing his third " lagging."

It is well known to the officers of the prison that the display of religion on his part, and that of many others, is a mere sham; that if they get the tip from their neighbours that the chaplain is in their neighbourhood, their Bible will be open on the table, or he will very likely find them on their knees, but as soon as he is gone they will be indulging in obscene conversation through their "chat-holes." I am sorry to have to insist that this religious trickery and deceit is made to pay.

One of the ways of fetching an "easy lagging" is to be a canter and a hypocrite. The prisoners know this, and so there is in every convict prison a whole regiment enlisted under the "banner of the Cross." Many of them have been praying and singing and "communing" through two or three "laggings.". When their present sentence expires they will take a "spell." They will stop praying and take to thieving, until the "bobby" catches them at their old tricks, when they will return to penal servitude to pray and sing and "commune" again, and so fetch another "easy lagging."

I hope that in making these strictures I shall not be misunderstood. God forbid that I should throw a stone at any religious professions which are sincere, and the genuineness of which are borne out in the life of the professor. I have a real respect for the adherents of any creed, no matter how absurd I may think its tenets, if belief in them ensures purity of life. No creed can be wholly bad if it produces good men. I know—few better than I—that nothing but misery and wretchedness attend the steps of those who stray from the path of *true* godliness. I know that it is only by a consciousness that we are ever in the sight of a great Eternal Father, who makes virtue its own reward, that we can hope to avoid impurity and sin. I know also that it is only by sincere and hearty repentance of misdeeds, and a fixed determination to live henceforth in honesty, and sobriety, and truth, and in the fear of the good God, that any peace can come into a man's soul.

But while feeling all this, and having, I hope, realized, the truth of it in my own experience, I cannot help expressing the contempt and abhorrence which I feel for the cheats who attempt to palm themselves off upon the credulous as penitents and pietists, while their inner

life is so filthy and abominable as to make one
doubt their humanity. That thousands of convicts do this for the sake of the pettiest of petty
advantages I am quite certain, and the only way
to put an end to it is to prevent any favour being
shown to any prisoner on account of any religious
profession which he may make. No truly repen-
tant man will object to this, for such one would
be ashamed to accept immunity from labour for
simply doing his duty, and "walking humbly
with God."

The prison libraries are organized by the
chaplains, and are really under their control,
but of necessity the distribution is left to the
schoolmasters. There are good books in the
libraries, but it is fifty to one against the man
who can understand and appreciate a good book
getting it.

The grossest carelessness and want of discrimination characterise the action of the schoolmasters in this matter as in all others. The
don't-carishness which they exhibit is unpardonable. A boor who cannot read at all will be very
likely to get Macaulay's "Essays," or Hallam's

"Middle Ages," while an educated man, or a thinking man who desires to learn something, will be condemned to the one hundred and forty-ninth perusal of "Robinson Crusoe." The boor will probably lay Mr. Hallam upon his shelf and not trouble to put him out for exchange again for three months, and during that time fifty poor fellows are starving for mental food which might fit them for a better life. I believe that there is at Portland a copy of Motley's "Dutch Republic" and of some of Mr. Prescott's works, but although I made incessant applications for three years, I never obtained them, owing to the sheer inanity of the schoolmasters.

A tolerably good joke was current at Portland in my time. A "rural" prisoner, who, I suppose, did not come from "very far north," was anxious to obtain an amusing book. By the advice of his neighbour he made an application to see the chaplain. That functionary tapped at his door about a week afterwards to inquire what he wanted. He quite innocently requested that he might be supplied with "The Life and Adventures of the Three Lazy Schoolmasters." The chaplain doubtless chuckled to himself, and retailed the joke in the evening over his "beeswing," but the book was not forthcoming.

Two books I did get at Portland, which to me were invaluable. They contained gems of poetry and prose of which one never tires, and which, after I had committed them to memory, were to me a "continual feast." They were the "Half-Hours with the Best Authors," which was published by good old Charles Knight, and "The Cyclopædia of English Literature," published a few years ago by Messrs. Chambers. The only fault with the latter was, that amongst a host of selections which were pure gold, an unfair quantity of dross was mingled, evidently for no other reason than because it was *Scotch* dross. I gave all that "a wide berth" of course, and I then found sufficient to command my gratitude to the compilers.

Out of the sixteen hundred prisoners at Portland there are perhaps two hundred who can understand and appreciate such books as those I have named. The Rev. Mr. Hill, for many years, and until recently, the senior chaplain at that station, told me in 1876 that he had more than a hundred applications *at one time* for EACH of the books named, and an equal number for Boswell's "Johnson" and Scott's "Napoleon." Many of these were from illiterate prisoners to whom these books would be of no use, but who had an equal chance of obtaining them. Such books as the two first and the last I have named would certainly tend to improve the minds and raise the moral tone of the men who are anxious to read them, and would perhaps be of as much service in fitting them to do their duty and become useful members of society in this world, as are the "Dairyman's Daughter" and Baxter's "Saint's Rest" to prepare them for another. The last-named books are in abundance, of the former there is but a single copy of each in the library.

I do not want to intrude on the domain of the ecclesiastical powers, but I venture to submit that orthodoxy and mere outward conformity of the criminal class are not of so much importance to the State, as is their regeneration on this material and sublunary sphere. Let the law while it has them under control try to transform them into good, honest, intelligent citizens. After their release, if the parsons can induce them to adopt any of their peculiar isms, and those isms will keep them straight for the future, why, the community will owe a debt of gratitude both to the parsons and the isms.

There have been any number of books written which if read and studied would tend to make men good, and honest, and industrious, and pure in this world. Surely these are the characteristics of all the writings of one whom I consider the greatest of living authors, and who is perhaps the greatest of living men; yet not one of the productions of Thomas Carlyle can be found in any prison library. Harriet Martineau and Mr. Froude are excluded, and many other authors who have written with the object of improving and refining the race,—and why? For no other reason than that the authors named are too honest to say they believe what they do not believe, and are unable to digest all the antique orthodoxy of the "Fathers of the Church."

At Dartmoor I was very fortunate in getting

from the chaplain Mr. Froude's "Short Essays on Great Subjects," but it was only by a fluke. The chaplain had not had time to read them. No other prisoner got them, for they were condemned on account of some religious sentiment contained in them, not coinciding with his reverence's prejudices. I presume some censorship to be necessary, but would it not be better if it were placed in the hands of some liberal-minded man in London who could supervise all the books issued for the use of the prisoners? At present, books issued freely in one prison are forbidden in another.

I take it for granted that no long time will elapse before there is a classification of prisoners. When that arrangement is made, and when all those men who are not wholly given over to the devil are set apart from the habitual criminals, it would be a very wise provision to appoint for each prison two or three large-hearted men of high moral character, whose duty it would be to visit every prisoner in rotation, and converse with him during the hours not devoted to labour; or if the men worked in their cells, as I think they should do, the visits might be made while they are at work. This would obviate all the objections which are raised to the solitary system. It is not necessary to a man's sanity that he should be *always* talking; and such visits, and the expectation of such visits, would altogether prevent men from becoming melancholy and brooding over the idea that they are forgotten and uncared for.

At Portland there is one such man who is called the "Scripture-Reader," but as there are sixteen hundred men at that station, and as he is limited to one hour in the evening for making his visits, he is not able to see any prisoner very often. Mr. Gibbs, of whom I speak, is certainly the most useful man I saw in the service during my imprisonment. He had himself belonged to the industrial class; he is a conscientious total abstainer; and he was able and willing, as far as opportunity was allowed him, to give in a brotherly way sound advice to the prisoners.

I know of two or three instances in which

he was successful in inducing young and comparatively innocent men to avoid the company and language of the old thieves, and I know of one or two others whom drink had taken to prison, who, in consequence of his earnest advocacy, left prison with a determination to make their first call at the offices of a temperance society and sign the pledge.

Half-a-dozen such men, with unlimited opportunities of seeing and talking with young prisoners, might have effected an amount of good which cannot be over-estimated.

There are more than two hundred officers at Portland whose duty it is to guard and control the men; but, the chaplains having no time for this sort of exhortation, there is only this one man to point out to them that there is a more excellent way to pass through life than in spending it in debauchery and vice. I think the governor of Portland would soon discover that he could dispense with the services of a score or two of "screws" if he had half-a-dozen such men as Mr. Gibbs on his staff, and each one had ample opportunities to exercise his influence upon such prisoners as are impossible. At Dartmoor there is not even one of these readers and exhorters.

I commend this subject to the very serious attention of the Government. Then the young novices in crime instead of being contaminated by old thieves, and by them rendered unfit for ever to mix with honest or decent people, would be properly advised and guided, and would perchance leave prison with honest hearts, and become eventually useful members of the commonwealth.

There is another plan which, if adopted by the chaplains, would I am sure lead to good results. Let the men be assembled in the chapel on one evening in the week during the winter months, and addressed on some subject not altogether religious. There are doubtless many able and eloquent men who would, for the love of God and human progress, give their services, and address their fallen fellow-creatures on temperance and industry, and literature and science. If the chaplains object to the importation of outsiders let them do it themselves. I repeat there are men open to good influences, and if by some such means as I have indicated they could be rescued from the criminal life into which the other branches of the Convict Department seem to condemn them, it would be work worthy even the high vocation of a Christian minister.

CHAPTER VIII.

REPORT OF THE COMMISSION.

IT may savour of presumption for me to review the recent Report of the Commission, but at least I shall bring to it a practical knowledge of the subject upon which they have reported. The suggestions and recommendations which have emanated from Lord Kimberley and his associates are exceedingly valuable, and although they have left untouched the important question of education, and although they have not solved the two problems of how to diminish crime, and what to do with incorrigible and habitual criminals, they have yet presented Mr. Cross with a great deal of material towards his coming measure of prison reform.

My object in this chapter will be to offer some suggestions in regard to what has been recommended by the Commission, and also to try to supply some further material which, if considered, may be found worth the attention of the Secretary of State.

At section 29 the Commissioners speak of the nine months of separate confinement at Millbank and Pentonville, and intimate that, with the exception of attendance at chapel and exercise, the visits of the governor, medical officer, chaplain, or warder to the prisoner in his cell, alone break the silence and solitude of his life. This ought to be true: if responsible and reliable officers were employed, it would be true; and if it were true, and the system could be extended through the whole sentence of men convicted for the first time, they would, unless they really belong to the constitutionally vicious and incorrigible class, never be *re*-convicted, and would emerge into the world redeemed and reclaimed.

This is the opinion of every intelligent and educated convict with whom I have come in contact. I have not the most remote doubt of its truth; and if Mr. Cross can, before quitting the fatigues of office, persuade the Legislature to give solitary confinement a fair trial, I feel very sure that it will prevent many thousands from enlisting in the dreadful army of professional criminals. I am convinced that five years is too long a sentence for any man convicted for the first time, unless it be for some very heinous offence. Three or four years of solitary confinement would be found quite sufficient to prevent a novice from engaging again in crime; but even if the five years' rule be maintained, there is no good reason why the solitary system should not be tried. Some over-anxious and tender-hearted philanthropists have expressed fears that so long a period of silence and solitude would produce lunacy.

This could only be in the case of men with very weak minds, and such could be specially provided for by medical certificate. I know, and it is the experience of all whose opinion is worth consideration, that it was only when I was cut off from all society, and compelled to hold communion with myself, that I fully turned my thoughts inwards, and reflected upon the wickedness which had landed me in a convict's cell; and then it was, I formed resolves which, with

God's help, I hope will protect me in the future. It is argued that solitude renders men dull and morose. Well, men cannot be overcome with remorse for an ill-spent life, and feel at the same time particularly jolly.

If a man is to be reformed he must lament over his past misdoings; and when is he most likely to lament? When he is in the society of ribald and obscene jokers, who laugh with fiendish glee at whatever is pure or decent, or in the solitude of his cell, with only God and an accusing conscience? If men are to be humbled into that state of contrition which must necessarily precede reformation, there must be sorrow, and no doubt sorrow produces dejection.

Would it not be wise to encourage a little dejection, if by its operation thieves can be transformed into honest men? But all the evils of the separate system are easily obviated. Work, constant and earnest work, and books when the work is done, with the occasional visits of such men as Mr. Gibbs at Portland—men who will walk into a prisoner's cell and grasp his hand, and then sit down and show him how easy a thing it is for a man, with God's help, to be happy in this world if he is only honest and sober and true, and that even for men who have fallen ever so low there is hope, if they will but fearlessly defy the devil for the future. Such truths spoken earnestly by large-hearted men from time to time would to all but the most degraded prisoners, give food for reflection, preserve them from the extremes of melancholy, and inspire them with bright hopes for the future.

Then there is work to be done which, if earnestly pursued, would preserve men from overbrooding. As I have shown, the work now performed in prisons is not earnest work. No man will be made an industrious man, or be qualified to obtain an honest livelihood, by the work he does in prison: it would not buy him prison rations. If a man worked in his cell either at a loom or at shoemaking or tailoring, and was given to understand that he would be rewarded with the proceeds of his labour after a sufficiency had been earned for his maintenance, he would have an incitement to work; and if he really worked there would be no fear of such extreme dejection as could lead to lunacy. No doubt idleness takes many men to prison; the professional thief *won't work*; but amongst the other classes idleness is *fostered* in prison; every prisoner does as little as he possibly can because no reward is offered for his industry.

Let me here quote from a work published in the first half of this century, entitled "Self-Formation." The author, by the enunciation of self-evident truths, not only shows the importance and value of work in the abstract, but also proves that earnest work is an infallible remedy for all the evils which are supposed to be chargeable to solitary confinement.

He says, "I have heard and read repeatedly that idleness is a very great evil; but the censure does not appear to me to come up to the real truth. I begin to think that it is not only a very great evil, but the greatest evil, and not only the greatest one, but, in fact, the only one—the only *mental* one, I mean; for, of course, as to morality a man may be very active, and very viciously active too. But the one great sensible and conceivable evil is that of idleness. *No man is wretched in his energy.* There can be no pain in a fit; a soldier at the full height of his spirit, and in the heat of contest, is unconscious even of a wound; the orator in the full flow of rhetoric is altogether exempt from the pitifulness of gout and rheumatism. *To be occupied, in its first meaning, is to be possessed as by a tenant;* and see the significance of first meanings. *When the occupation is once complete, when the tendency is full, there can be no entry for any evil spirit; but idleness is emptiness; where it is, there the doors are thrown open and the devils troop in."*

Leaving out of the question the old and habitual criminals, I think the Government have here in a nutshell the only effective means for reforming criminals and turning them into honest men: —*Solitary confinement; no association with the re-convicted men; the occasional visit and counsel of earnest, practical advisers; and steady, earnest, unremitting labour,* which shall enable the convict to earn sufficient money to emigrate and begin a new life in a new land.

In sections 34 to 40, inclusive, the Commissioners describe the present system of classification—good-conduct marks, remission, and gratuities, without suggesting any reform. The existing scale of marks is a very peculiar invention. Under its provisions a prisoner is not credited with any marks during the first nine months of his sentence, no matter how good his conduct or how great his industry; but if he breaks any prison rule during the probationary period he is fined a certain number of marks, which are deducted from those he is expected to earn in the future.

Another anomaly is that after the close of the probationary period every prisoner is credited with six marks per day, no matter how bad his conduct or how great his indolence, but in earning only six marks per day he gets no remission. The six marks' credit, therefore, is a mere delusion; it means nothing, and endless trouble might be saved by giving good-conduct men one and two marks per day, and bad-conduct men none. The whole mark system is nevertheless a strong argument in favour of the classification of prisoners.

With the present class of men who are employed as warders, eight marks per day does not at all mean good conduct and steady hard labour; indeed, the amount of work done is not taken into account by one officer in twenty. It means that the prisoner has given the officer in charge of him no trouble; that he has not bothered him at all; that he has not even troubled him for anything which would have helped him to do more work; and that he has kept his eyes open to give his supervisor the "tip" in case of the approach of a superior officer. These are, in practice, the things which obtain a man his full number of marks, and it may be readily conceived that the majority of those who obtain in this way their full remission and are the soonest let loose to prey again upon the public are the old thieves that are up to all prison dodges, who are thoroughly posted up as to when it is safe to break a rule and when it is not, and who "know their way about" generally.

Now, I would suggest that re-convicted men should not only be kept in distinct prisons, but should be deprived of the privilege of earning remission. There certainly ought not to be any great hurry about liberating men who have given ample proof that they intend to live always by plunder. There are two very effective ways of keeping these habitual thieves in order—bread-and-water diet and the whip; they hate both as much as the devil hates holy water.

At clause 38 the Commissioners speak of the amount awarded to prisoners on their release.

The necessity which exists for a classification of prisoners is at no time more apparent than on the occasion of a convict's discharge. Three pounds is not much to give a man with which to begin the world. However sincere may be the convict's aspirations for a life of industry and honour, he is in most cases destitute of friends who can aid him to obtain employment. If he is to be honest, a little help from the Government is necessary to provide him with the implements of industry; and yet, so long as all classes of prisoners are subject to the same regulations, I could not conscientiously advise the Government to increase the amount of gratuity.

All that I heard from the men who were

awaiting their discharge from Millbank contemporaneously with myself, and the resolutions I heard expressed by hundreds of men upon public works, as to what would be their first action upon their release, forces me to the conclusion that in the case of two-thirds of all the convicts, the amount paid to them, whether it were three pounds or thirty, would go to swell the receipts of some old acquaintance who sells intoxicating liquors.

The same argument applies to the clothes in which prisoners are discharged. And this brings me to clause 41. The Commissioners state that improvements have been made in quality and fashion. I shall speak my own experience. The "togs" in which I was "rigged out" were an advertisement to the police, and to the public. There was, to all intents and purposes, an announcement upon my back that I was a "ticket-of-leave man."

Such an arrangement may seem suited for all old gaol-birds and irreclaimables. If three-fourths of the convicts who are discharged were attired in a respectable and serviceable suit of clothes, at a cost of three or four pounds, the result would be, that after an entire outfit had been obtained from Petticoat-lane for about five-and-sixpence, the clothes supplied by the Government would be consigned to the care of their uncle for twelve calendar months, and at the expiration of the year would be knocked down to the highest bidder by some auctioneer.

In my own case, and in that of others similarly situated, I think there is cause for complaint. As I have admitted, the act which consigned me to prison admits of no apology and deserves no excuse; still, I was not a gaol-bird, or an habitual criminal, and shall be much more likely to offer myself as food to the sharks that haunt the Portland breakwater than to seek re-admission into the ranks of the convicts who built it.

On my advent to Pentonville, the authorities took possession of a suit of clothes adapted to my position in life, and which had shortly before cost me twelve or fourteen pounds. On my release I was turned loose in a suit, the shoddiness of which is itself a lesson in rascality, and in which I should have been quite ashamed to seek employment in my own profession. The contract price of the material may have been ten shillings, and it was botched together as only prison tailors can botch. Its value was *nil;* a good sharp shower would reduce it to a rag : no, not even to a rag, for it was shoddy. It is simply a fair-weather covering for a man's nakedness for a month, if he is very careful and does no work.

After two hours' wear, having in the meantime obtained possession of some of the auxiliaries of civilization, and being anxious to be rid of everything that smacked of the prison, I offered the suit for sale to one of the "sons of Zebedee;" he said "It was no goot," and he was perfectly right. He thought he might be able to "palm it off upon a flat," and he would risk a crown for it. I accepted his offer with thanks, and immediately put several streets between myself and the last relics of prison life.

I fancy I hear some sagacious reader ask whether the *Royal Society for the Aid of Discharged*

Prisoners does not fill the vacuum left by the Government. I would preface my reply with a suggestion that there should be no vacuum. The class of men who would appreciate a little help on their release, and to whom it would really be useful, should be instigated to industry during their term of imprisonment by the promise of remuneration for any amount of work they could perform beyond their allotted task. This being no part of the Government programme, the Society might, if properly managed, play the part of "Good Samaritan," towards men who are anxious to work their way back into respectability. I have taken some pains to ascertain whether it has assumed this great and humane character.

I cannot hear of many cases in which it has been really useful in serving its unfortunate clients. It appears to be a mere bank in which a man can deposit the small sum allowed him by the Government and receive it back in driblets. The majority of discharged prisoners have relatives or friends who, however poor, will give them food or shelter for a week or two, and they hang about the offices of the Society day after day for two or three hours, to obtain the trifle which is doled out to them, and which trifle they too often swallow in the shape of beer. The bonus which is added by the Society is given only to those men who come to them with a sheet upon which there is no record of any infraction of the prison rules; and, as I have explained elsewhere, the men who are best able to avoid report are the experienced professional thieves. But gratuity and bonus do not amount to much, and are soon exhausted. The object of the Society should be to lay out the amount promptly in some way which would enable the man to earn a living; or else to obtain immediate employment for him, and expend the money in the purchase of those necessary comforts which will enable him to pursue his avocation without anxiety.

I would take the liberty to suggest to the generous and philanthropic Duke of Westminster, who is President of this Royal Society, that a committee of shrewd and benevolent men of business, who would take an interest in promoting the objects for which the Society was founded, and who would in turn give their services to inquire into the nature of the requirements, as well as into the true character and disposition of the applicants, would be a far more effective machine for accomplishing good than an expensive "figure-head" and a staff of red-tape officials of the policeman class, whose interests are concentrated in the salaries which they draw from this well-intentioned engine of benevolence, and whose humane instincts are controlled by official routine.

Section 41 refers to the surveillance of prisoners discharged on licence. Unfortunately this bears most heavily and unequally upon the most innocent class. The well-intentioned man, whose desire for the future is to be law-abiding and industrious, gets into a respectable neighbourhood, furnishes his correct address to the authorities, and tries to get work. Very often the fact that his whereabouts and antecedents are known at the police-station nearest his residence, and to the police employed upon that beat, operate most injuriously upon the man's interests and chances of work.

Policemen are naturally anxious to show their acuteness and activity to their superiors, and the man with honest intentions is often foiled in his attempts to gain an honest living by the assiduity of the police. If he is honest, all his actions and movements are open and above-board, and he is easy game for policemen who desire to exhibit their 'cuteness by unearthing a ticket-of-leave man. The thief gives the address of some chum, who is prepared at all times with an answer to inquiries, and successfully eludes police vigilance. I entirely acquit the Criminal Investigation Department of all blame. If they had it in their power to appoint half-a-dozen men of education and acuteness, who had sufficient judgment to discriminate between the different classes of prisoners discharged, and to keep their eye upon them without opening their mouths unnecessarily, the honest and industrious man would be able to work his way back to respectability without impediment, and the man who has gone back to thieving would be more readily caged. Such officers, however, could not be hired for policemen's pay, and in this matter the authorities are economical in the wrong place.

I never forget a face, and in my walks about

London I continually see men whom I knew in prison, who are evidently bent on mischief. I think that if I had charge of a certain number of the men discharged in London, saw them on the morning of their discharge, and knew their registered address, I should be able in a month to make a reliable report to the authorities as to their proclivities and habits, and to classify the innocent and the guilty. There can be no doubt that for a reasonable remuneration competent officers could be obtained to do this, and the result would be the protection and safety of the reformed and industrious man, and the *rapid* reconviction of the rogue.

In sections 70 to 74 the Commissioners review and admit the existence of the evils I have pointed out as to the contamination of young offenders by hardened criminals.

Clause 75 suggests the real and only remedy, and it is so important and wise a suggestion that I give it in its entirety :—" It has been suggested as a remedy, that a sentence to separate imprisonment might be adopted as a substitute or alternative for the present sentence of five years' penal servitude. We may assume that a less period of imprisonment than three years could not be regarded as an equivalent for five years' penal servitude; and the first question which arises is, whether prisoners could be detained in separate confinement for so long a period without risk of injury to their mental and bodily health. In Belgium criminals are subjected to cellular imprisonment for much longer periods, and, it is said, without injury; but without laying too much stress on the Belgian practice, concerning which we have not full information, we may point out that it does not appear that prisoners have suffered unduly from imprisonment in the county and borough gaols, in some of which the system of separation has been enforced for periods usually not exceeding eighteen months, but sometimes extending to two years. Upon the whole we are of opinion that, with certain relaxations during the latter part of the sentences, such as longer hours of exercise, more frequent schooling, and visits from chaplains and Scripture-readers, more books and more time allowed for reading, more frequent communications with their families by letters and visits, all of which, however, it must be borne in mind, would materially diminish the severity of the punishment, prisoners might be confined in separate cells without serious risk for as much as three years." But, unfortunately, the Commissioners do not recommend the adoption of this excellent plan.

Clause 76 says:—" The introduction of such a sentence into our criminal code would have the undoubted advantage that a considerable number of criminals, and especially of the less-hardened class, would be withdrawn from the danger of contamination by associating with other convicts. But, notwithstanding this advantage, we have come to the conclusion, after carefully weighing the arguments which have been adduced on both sides, that it is not desirable to make so vital a change in our penal system." The efficacy of the cure is admitted, but its adoption is not recommended because it is a *vital change*. Surely it is a vital change which is needed. The Commissioners fear that the difference between the two years' sentence and the three would not be sufficiently marked, and that the dread of it would not be so great as of the five years' sentence. Now the present two years' sentence is in practice eighteen months. Three years would be the double of eighteen months, and it might be understood that a man receiving that sentence would have to complete his three years. If three years of solitary confinement with hard and constant work, good books and instruction, and wise advisers will not reform a man, will any sentence do it? Will twenty years do it? I am convinced that it will not; and I think that those of Her Majesty's Judges who have taken any interest in watching the career of criminals will entirely agree with me.

The object of the law is to punish, but it is also to reform the offender. If in three years an offender can be made an honest and industrious man, why should the State be longer burdened with his care, and why should the commonwealth be any longer deprived of a wealth-producer? If in the sequel he proves incorrigible, he will soon be re-convicted, and should then be treated as an habitual criminal, and deprived for a very long time of the power of preying upon the community.

I have carefully studied the character of the different classes of convicts amongst whom I have been thrown, and I am certain that by the system suggested in this 75th clause, one-half of the men now convicted would, instead of being contaminated and turned into brutes, be transformed into honest, and sober, and reasonable beings. Why not try it?

In clauses 78 and 79, the Commissioners recommend a plan of classification, which I admit would be an improvement in the present plan, but not a *great* and effectual improvement. They suggest the classification of prisoners into classes according to the nature of the crimes for which they are undergoing punishment, or the formation into a separate class of those against whom no previous conviction is known to have been recorded. There are fatal objections to both these plans, some of which the Commissioners set forth themselves in another clause.

An old and hardened receiver of stolen goods,

who has had a run of luck for twenty years and at last gets caught, is not a fit associate or tutor for noviciates in crime. I have met with many old pickpockets, thieves of the worst class, who have moved rapidly about the country for many years and escaped detection. These men, thorough adepts at their trade, and able to boast of a long career of undetected crime, would be the very worst associates for men who are *really* first offenders, and yet they would be eligible for that class.

It is not only that first offenders are often very bad men, and convicted of very heinous crimes, but that men convicted for the first time are often experienced thieves, who have escaped detection because of their extraordinary dexterity and expertness : surely these would be the very worst companions for new beginners. Would they not urge, as they have often done to me, that if a thief is a " wide " man he need not get caught, and that it was carelessness, and not keeping his eyes open, that gets him " nabbed "?

There is an old man now at Portland who was

known amongst thieves as "the badger." He worked side by side with me on the works, and I learned a good deal of his history from his own lips. I remember his joining our party on the morning after his arrival from Woking. He was immediately recognised by three professional thieves in our gang, who hailed from "the smoke," which was his name for London.

He seemed to be very popular amongst his old acquaintance, and was pronounced by them all to be a "square man." He was a notorious "fence." He had been buying stolen goods and furnishing the necessary implements for burglaries for more than forty years, but had until now succeeded in eluding the vigilance of the police. He told me himself that he always had "wonderful luck" in discovering "good plants," or, in other words, "spotting" places where burglarious entrances could be made and something worth having found. The "badger" told me that there was scarcely an "eminent" thief in London with whom he was not acquainted, and I am very sure that there were few of the tricks of his trade in which he was not proficient.

I knew another man who, amongst thieves, took the position of an aristocrat. His name was Shrimpton, and he was famous amongst his "chums" as having been the hero of a hundred successful burglaries. He had reduced lock-picking and safe-breaking to a science, and, unlike most thieves, had out of the proceeds of his infamy provided for his family a comfortable home. He resided at Brixton, and I have reason to believe that his family were well-educated and well-clothed and fed. Yet this man was without private means, and had never in his life engaged in any honest industrial pursuit. He was a constitutional and scientific robber, yet so clever that he was only detected for the first time when he was nearly sixty years of age.

Another fellow whom I met, and who was the hero of a long career of undetected crime, hailed from Birmingham. He assured me that for twenty years he had made heaps of money by hotel robberies in the Midland counties, and that he never allowed an excursion-train to leave Birmingham without obtaining half-a-dozen purses and a watch or two from travellers who were bustling to obtain seats. He was at Portland under his first sentence of penal servitude.

Now, such men as these should, of course, be classified as old thieves.

I can imagine no influence so bad upon those who are *really* first offenders as that of the heroes who have for years succeeded in evading justice, and to this influence these first offenders would still be exposed if the recommendation of the Commissioners were adopted. Is there a better plan, or one more likely to be effectual and to succeed, than solitary confinement with shorter sentences, harder work, incentives to industry in the shape of a reward which will give the man a start at the close of his imprisonment, and all this to be accompanied by some sensible efforts for the man's intellectual and moral reform? I think there is no other way; but it is a subject well-worthy the consideration of statesmen.

Clause 102 refers to the prison dietary. I have already said that I think it needs but little change. For men employed at indoor labour it is ample, men employed in the open air might, perhaps with advantage, be allowed a few additional ounces of bread. There are gluttons, of course, who would never have enough, and, as the Commissioners state, there are degraded animals amongst the convicts with such depraved voracity, that they will, and would under any circumstances, gorge themselves with any kind of filth which comes in their way. In the prisons where candles are used it is quite a common thing for the prisoners to eat their candles and sit in the dark.

In the party with which I worked at Portland there were half-a-dozen men who fed themselves daily upon snails, slugs, and frogs, and they did this not only without any interference on the part of the officer in charge, but to his evident amusement. I was for a short time attached to a party at Portland whose duty it was to drag a cart about to collect ashes and rubbish from the different departments of the prison. It was considered by a certain class of prisoners quite a privilege to be attached to the "cart party," on account of the refuse food and poultices which could be fished out of the infirmary ashes. To men of this class no diet would be sufficient, but it may be asserted with confidence that the prison fare served out to them is better in quality, more cleanly, and of larger quantity than they have been accustomed to enjoy in the places which they call their homes. It is not wonderful that when so large a number of convicts feed themselves upon disgusting garbage of all sorts, the prison doctor should be so constantly in demand. As I have before intimated, his position is one of great responsibility and delicacy, and the Commissioners, in clauses 110 to 112, make some very wise and sensible recommendations with reference to the selection of thoroughly-qualified practitioners.

In clause 119, the Commissioners speak of the dark iron cells at Portsmouth and Dartmoor, and admit the existence of all the evils which I have described in connection with them—their darkness, the facilities they give for communication, and their other evils. I do not know whether the Commissioners visited Portland, which is, I believe, the largest of all the convict stations; but they make no mention in their report of the cells there. There are at Portland seven distinct prisons or halls, each one accommodating about an equal number of prisoners. In the seven prisons the whole of the cells are of corrugated iron, and offer the facilities for communication which I have described. Certainly in nine out of every ten cells, holes have been bored to render talking more easy; and in exactly half of all the cells in five of the prisons the cells are so dark, that reading, except by gaslight, is quite impossible.

At clause 132, the Report refers to the infliction of corporal punishment. I quite agree with the author of "Five Years' Penal Servitude," that there are a class of convicts who dread no other punishment than this. Every Englishman will be glad to see the soldiers and sailors of England relieved from liability to so degrading a punishment; but if my readers will refer to the description I have given of the character of large numbers of the convicts, they will perhaps perceive that these men cannot be humiliated, and that nothing can add to their degradation. They have no moral sensibilities, appeals to their reason would be of no avail, and as to their conscience, I do not fancy they have known its voice for many a long day. There is one thing, and *only* one thing, of which they stand in mortal dread—the cat.

Many of them care nothing about loss of marks, and in fact prefer to do all their sentences, because they are released from police supervision: loss of food they do not like; but the *cat* is their mortal aversion. I must do the authorities the justice to say that I have never seen it resorted to except for heinous offences; but I am quite sure that if its use were abolished there are a certain class of prisoners who would be quite uncontrollable. All sorts of brutal violence towards both prisoners and officers would be common but for the fear of the lash. I know this from the admissions of the men themselves. A strong proof of its deterrent effects occurs to me.

It has been a custom for many years at Portland for the prisoners to sing songs in their cells on Christmas-night. So long as this custom was kept within bounds it was to a certain extent tolerated; but at Portland the evil grew more obnoxious and unbearable every year. On the Christmas of 1876 all sorts of vulgar, indecent, and beastly songs were sung aloud, and the prison reverberated with obscene and disgusting language, shouts of defiance to the authorities, and the free use of damnatory epithets. On the following day a good many men were reported and subjected to bread-and-water punishment, loss of marks, &c. This had no effect whatever.

On the Christmas-night of 1877 the same game was not only repeated, but in the prison called F north, in which the Roman Catholic prisoners are located, the blasphemous and obscene language and the filthy and disgusting songs were beyond all description horrible and hellish. Mr. Clifton was called up after midnight, and was himself a witness of what was going on. He carefully and very properly satisfied himself of the identity of a score of the worst offenders, and at the next visit of the director, and on the recommendation of the governor, these men got "two dozen."

On the Christmas-night of 1878 perfect order and quiet reigned throughout the prison. Comment is unnecessary. The only wonder is, that with undoubted evidence before them of what is the only punishment which these pests of society dread, the judges and prison authorities do not more often resort to it.

In clause 142, the Commissioners refer to the question of evidence given by warders against prisoners for breaking rules. It is no doubt the fact that a great many men are punished on the testimony of officers, the men being entirely innocent of what is charged against them; and, for the reasons I have given in another place, unprincipled officers make scapegoats of the most guileless class of prisoners, and almost never of "second timers" and old thieves, who, on the other hand, enjoy their confidence. This evil can only be effectually cured by the exercise of more care in the selection of officers, and by paying them better.

It would be of course dangerous to take the evidence of prisoners against officers, for I regret to say that mendacity is so very general amongst convicts, that it is considered quite the right thing for a man to say *anything* which will gain his end. I think, however, that the evil might be somewhat checked if officers were compelled always to give their testimony upon oath. There must, I think, be some, even amongst the worst class of officers, who would hesitate to swear to a lie; though from my experience of others, I fear they would not hesitate to carry their point even if they had to swear upon a whole stack of Bibles. There can be no doubt that vice is infectious, and I believe that a large number of prison officials, being themselves destitute of a very high morality, have from long association not only imbibed the slang and the mendacity, but some other of the bad qualities of habitual thieves. Convict prisons are Augean stables, which require a great deal of cleansing in all their departments.

At clause 147 the Commissioners, speaking of the custom of corrupt officials making money by supplying prisoners with tobacco, recommend that officers should be subjected to a search similar to that adopted in the Custom-House. It does not seem to have occurred to them that in public-works prisons this would not remedy the evil at all. The custom both at Portland and Dartmoor was for the officer to "plant" the supplies of tobacco upon the works outside the prison. This the warder could do in the evening after his duties were over and he had left the prison, or in the early morning. The prisoner was of course informed where it was deposited. If the *customer* happened to be employed inside the prison walls, it was always easy for him to find a chum in a neighbouring cell who worked out-of-doors, and who would for a consideration act as his agent and carrier. The only remedy for this in public-works prisons is in the selection of a better class of officers.

It may, perhaps, interest the directors of the convict department to know that, at Portland, a large quantity of tobacco finds its way into the prison which does not come through the hands of the officers. I was once at work near a cluster of huts, which were occupied by serjeants and corporals of the Engineer corps.

The wives of these men, actuated by the kindest of motives, were accustomed to throw pieces of tobacco at night where they knew the prisoners would find them in the morning. I did not care for the tobacco, but I must plead guilty to having once found a jam tart, carefully wrapped up in a London evening paper of the previous day. I relished the tart, but I gloated over the newspaper. By-the-by I loaned that newspaper to another prisoner, who was careless enough to get caught with it, and was reported. On his appearance before the governor, that gentleman, on inspecting the date, exclaimed, "Dear me, you get your news almost as soon as I do. You will have three days and forfeit eighty-four marks."

Then the men connected with the Artillery corps are good-natured sometimes, and prisoners are able to make a much cheaper arrangement with them than with prison warders. The market price of cavendish tobacco obtained through a "screw" is ten shillings per pound, and even then he furnishes the very commonest description. Then it must be remembered that, when he obtains the usual five-pound note from the prisoner's friends, it is the rule that he should take half for running the risk; so that, including his profit on the tobacco, he gets four pounds out of the five. If a prisoner chooses to trust a soldier, he gets his business transacted on more liberal terms.

There is still another class at Portland who drive a trade amongst the "lags." There are several free men employed upon the works in charge of horses, which are necessary for the removal of trucks along the trams. These men are not paid directly by the department, but by contractors who furnish the horses. They earn about fourteen shillings a week,—high wages for Dorsetshire, but not so high as to make them fight shy when a sovereign is to be made out of a "lag." I recollect two very good old fellows. One was short of an arm and the other of a leg; they both had large families to support, and the only chance they had of providing a good dinner now and then for the bairns was by indulging in a little illicit trade with the "lags."

In other clauses the Commissioners in referring to the labour of convicts allude incidentally to the popular delusion that there is some injustice to the industrial classes in allowing the results of convict labour to come in competition with free labour. Now, of course care should be taken, on all accounts, that no articles produced should be sold for less than the market price, but taking for granted that this is done, no injustice would be done to any individual by making convict labour remunerative and profitable. It should be remembered that all these convicts ought to belong to the industrial classes, and that if they were doing their duty they would be taking their fair share in the labour of the country, earning their bread by the sweat of their brow, and adding to the wealth and prosperity of the country. Why, in the name of common sense, should they not be made to do this in prison?

Again, if all the convicts were earning their subsistence, the reduction in taxation would far more than compensate for the infinitesimally small difference which their added labour might make in the wages paid for the articles they manufactured. There are between thirty and forty millions of people in these islands, but, fearfully large as is the number of convicts, there are of the latter not fifteen thousand. One-half of these are too lazy, or too impotent to work, and the labour of the remainder, even if it were made, as it should be, remunerative and profitable, would make no sensible difference to the industrial classes.

The Commissioners suggest many valuable reforms, but there is only one other upon which I think it is necessary to comment. I mean the recommendation that suitable persons should be appointed to visit and inspect the convict prisons, and overrule and rectify the mistakes made by governors. As I have said in a former chapter, there is now an expensive machinery in the shape of a board of directors, which is almost valueless. It is chiefly composed of men who have been governors of convict prisons, and who are wedded to the stereotyped abuses connected with their management. The Commissioners recommend that some suitable gentlemen, members of Parliament or otherwise, who would volunteer for the office, should be appointed to visit and inspect the prisons. The suggestion is a most valuable one, but I adhere to the opinion I have expressed before that the present board of directors should be superseded by some one responsible head, whose prejudices should not be too favourable to the governors, and who should occupy his time in visiting all the prisons, and making a careful and conscientious investigation of all abuses and complaints.

The advantage to the community of the Criminal Investigation Department, under the able management of Mr. Howard Vincent, cannot be over-estimated. He will, no doubt, if not over-ruled, originate reforms which will bring the criminal class under more direct control. If a man of similar energy, ability, and conscientiousness were selected to supervise the prisons, I have no doubt that a marked reform would soon exhibit itself in the *morale* of both officers and prisoners.

CHAPTER IX.

SUGGESTIONS AND SUMMARY.

IN what I have said in the preceding chapters I have not shown sympathy with crime or with the criminal class. I certainly feel none. My object has been to show that the law has to deal with a large number of prisoners who do not belong to the absolutely criminal class, and that to these men it is at present acting unwisely and unjustly. It is not only in the interests of the prisoners that I have argued thus, but chiefly in the interests of society. Thieves are a pest and a plague to the whole community; and if I have proved, as I think I have, that convict prisons are at present high schools of crime, and manufactories for thieves, then, believing as I do that statesmen of both political parties are desirous to remedy abuses when they have found them, I have great confidence that measures will shortly be taken to remedy the evils I have pointed out.

I know that it is very easy to find fault, but fortunately there are no serious obstacles in the way of reform. Sir Wilfrid Lawson, in his crusade against public-houses, has to contend with vested interests. He has to fight against a well-disciplined phalanx of brewers and publicans whose interests are directly opposed to his success. Here there is nothing of the sort. In the reform I seek, the interest of every man, woman, and child in the community is directly concerned. I ask the Government to take all those stray sheep who, under the influence of drink or ignorance or poverty have wandered out of the highway of honour, and teach them that their own interests are identified with sobriety and honest industry. If it be true, and it surely is, that instead of doing this the Government is now allowing men of this class to be tutored by old thieves in all those cunning arts which will qualify them to be professional marauders in the future, why I need add no argument to show that the reform should be prompt and searching.

First of all, then, it is necessary that there should be a classification of prisoners, and in this matter great discrimination should be exercised. There are a great many prisoners who do not belong to the criminal class, and who yet have been previously convicted of some petty offence. This is especially true of the agricultural class. Giles's record shows that he once had a month for assaulting the police when he was drunk, and, what is worse than all in the view of Quarter Sessions magnates, he has once been convicted of consorting with poachers. Down the poor fellow goes for seven years, most likely the best seven years of his life.

Take another case, that of an educated man who has once been convicted of a trifling misdemeanour, and has been sentenced to pay a fine or go to prison in default. He pays the fine, but the conviction is registered against him. At a later period of his life he commits a not very heinous offence under the pressure of poverty. It is felony; his old peccadillo is hunted up by the police, and he gets seven years.

Now, I think that common sense says that twelve months of solitary confinement, with strict discipline and good reformatory treatment, might make reputable citizens of such men; but if the taxpayers are to be saddled with the cost of their families in the workhouses, and themselves in the convict prisons, for seven years, the Government should not herd them with the professional criminal class to which they do not belong, and with which, although they have broken the law, they have no sympathy. These men may safely be classed with any men who are sentenced to penal servitude for the first time and have had *no* previous conviction; and they are equally amenable to good influences.

The important question now arises, What is to be done with incorrigible thieves? I have suggested that three or four years of solitary confinement and hard work, accompanied by good educational, moral, and religious training, will reform a man if his reform be possible. I do not think the Government need trouble themselves about the contamination of re-convicted men who have undergone such a training. They are, practically, incorrigible, and it becomes the duty of the State to take care that they shall not again become a pest to society. Why should men who have had a fair chance, and yet give proof that they do not intend to exist except by plunder, be let loose again upon the community?

I would recommend that men who have once gone through the probation of solitary confinement should, upon re-conviction, receive a long sentence, and that during the sentence they should, if not physically incapable, be kept at hard and remunerative labour. It is admitted that except at Dartmoor there will, in three years from this, be no out-door employment at any of the existing stations. Now, what is to prevent the Government from employing these incorrigible thieves in mining operations? If I am not mistaken there are estates of the Crown in Cornwall and elsewhere which might be made available, and beyond doubt there is mineral wealth in Scotland and in Ireland which is only waiting to be unearthed.

My idea is that up to now the Government have been too tender in their care of incorrigible thieves. Granted that mining is arduous and dangerous work, why should we be more careful of the lives and limbs of men who have given ample proof that they respect neither life nor property than we are of the lives and limbs of our honest and industrious fellow-countrymen, who from childhood to old age toil on in honest industry, not only bearing their own burdens, but contributing to the general wealth and prosperity of their country? Echo answers—Why?

It is a mistake to suppose that habitual thieves have any dread of penal servitude in its present form. Of course they do their best to elude the vigilance of the police, because their highest notion of happiness in this world is to be free, in order that they may prey upon society and spend the proceeds in debauchery and drunkenness; but if caught and sentenced to penal servitude it its present form, they can, to use their own expression, "do it on their heads." Let them understand that they would have to "do it on their heads" in a coal-mine, with an occasional taste of the "cat" as an incentive to industry, and take my word for it a very large number would be most anxious to give penal servitude a very wide berth. I presume the Government to be anxious to abate crime, and I do not ask them to make the lot of these re-convicted men harder than that of tens of thousands of our honest fellow-countrymen. Why not give the experiment a trial?

The question will then arise as to what is to be done with them after ten or fifteen years of mining. Well, I think the community should still be protected against them. I see no objection to compulsory emigration. An island colony might easily be found where, if they were willing to till the ground, they could obtain a subsistence. Let the Government furnish them with the implements of labour, and with the necessary means to raise the first crop, and let them be given to understand that they would have to live under the "royal law" that if a man will not work neither shall he eat. The island might be under military law, which would summarily punish offenders. If they determined still to be birds of prey they could only prey upon each other, and would cease to be a curse and a nuisance to honest men. I know that this recommendation is revolutionary, but if by a revolution in this matter the thief class could within the next twenty years be reduced two-thirds, would it not be a wise and wholesome and economical revolution? I have entire faith in its success.

I have studied the character of this thief class, and I am certain that if they had the punishments I have depicted in prospect, they would try to escape them, and as a last resource perhaps actually resort to honest labour, for the means to live.

The Commissioners at the end of their recent Report summarised their recommendations. Let me follow their example :—

1. That in order to prevent contamination of the less-hardened convicts by old and habitual

offenders, or by those who perpetrate enormous or unnatural crimes, distinct prisons should be provided for them, and a special reformatory discipline instituted.

2. That it is advisable this class of prisoner should receive shorter sentences; and that as it is all but impossible to decide what prisoners are morally infectious, the system should be solitary confinement.

3. That the work of this class of prisoner should if possible be done in his cell, and under the supervision of properly-qualified officers of undoubted integrity.

4. That in order to relieve the monotony of the prison life, and at the same time to afford the prisoner opportunities for obtaining good counsel and intellectual food, he should at convenient times receive constant visits from the chaplain and from properly-qualified readers.

5. That it is advisable to give to the uneducated more ample opportunities to acquire instruction and improvement by tuition, by good books regularly and appropriately dis-

tributed, and by periodical lectures during the winter.

6. That it would be wise in the chaplains to urge practical godliness rather than doctrinal religion, to take care that no prisoner makes capital out of professions of piety, and to cease the administration of sacramental mysteries to men who it is well known accept them from improper and impure motives.

7. That while the work done by the prisoner should be earnest and unremitting, and calculated to fit him for a life of industry, it should also be remunerative to himself; and that as an incentive to industry the prisoner should clearly understand that the amount he is to receive on discharge will depend upon the amount of work he has accomplished.

8. That on discharge, a prisoner of this class should receive serviceable clothes of good quality, adapted to his station in life and the trade he seeks employment in.

9. That the supervision of discharged men should be entrusted to discreet and acute officers

of good judgment and education, who would protect and encourage those whom they found pursuing a life of honest industry, and seek the rapid re-conviction of incorrigible thieves.

10. That it is advisable that officers entrusted with the control of convicts should be selected with more care and discrimination than are at present exercised; and that it would be wise to appoint in the place of the present directors some one responsible head, who would visit and supervise all the prisons, and carefully report and remedy all abuses.

11. That, in addition to this alteration, it would be well to adopt the recommendation of the Commissioners as to the appointment of Visitors unconnected with the Convict Department, and unpaid.

12. That it is advisable to render the lives of determined and habitual thieves who are re-convicted more distasteful to them, and that it would be wise to employ them in arduous labour, which should be made remunerative to the State.

Lastly. That in view of the fact, that the

number of professional thieves is largely on the increase, it is advisable to lessen the evil by providing for the compulsory emigration, after a certain number of years of labour, of re-convicted men, and their location on some island where they would have no opportunity to rob the honest and industrious; and where, if again convicted, they could be dealt with summarily by the infliction of corporal punishment under military law.

I may mention, as against the probable argument that this last recommendation could not be carried out, that the Emperor of Brazil has adopted this very system, and with eminent success.

POSTSCRIPT.

THE Report of the Directors of the Convict Department for 1878 was issued whilst this work was in the Press. In it there is an evident attempt made to whitewash the present system, with the view of preventing any radical change. In reference to it I will only say that all the evils described in this work existed in full force, not only during the year to which the Report has reference, but after its publication at the end of September, 1879.

There is in the Report an intimation that in order to provide labour for convicts it will be necessary to inaugurate some new public works. The construction of a harbour at Filey Bay upon the east coast is hinted at. I am not prepared to say that such a work is not a great national requirement; but I think that it would be well for the guardians of the public purse to keep their eyes open, in order that no scheme may be adopted for the mere purpose of *creating* labour for convicts. If more millions are to be spent in these hard times, it should surely be in works for which there is a real necessity, and which would benefit the whole community.

I would also suggest that whatever may be the new field of labour, it will provide a good opportunity for removing from the existing prisons two or three thousand of old thieves who have been convicted for a second or third time.

This would be one important step towards the separation of the whole brood of habitual criminals from men of whom there may be some hope, and who are not altogether abandoned and incorrigible.

In the *Times* newspaper of September 30th, also published after this work was in the Press, an able editorial thus comments upon the system which has engendered the evils depicted in these pages:—" The fact is indisputable that convict prisons are excellent cages, but very indifferent reformatories. The Royal Commission has pointed out a defect in the classification of prisoners, which is partly accountable for the melancholy failure. The graduates in crime love their art, and console themselves, like a lame actor or a hoarse tenor, with teaching it to freshmen. Hitherto no attempt has been made to separate habitual offenders from beginners. A consequence known to all the world, except perhaps the Home Office, has been that the prisons educate as many professional criminals as the receivers of stolen goods."

Referring to the proposed new works at Filey Bay the same writer remarks:—" The directors suggest, as a mode of meeting the want, that a harbour at Filey Bay or elsewhere might be dug by convict labour, or that a large convict farm might be commenced. A prison would have to be built in the neighbourhood of the works. Such a prison could hardly be monopolized by prisoners convicted for the first time. Habitual offenders require outdoor labour as much at least as their juniors. There is, however, no necessity for the erection of two prisons, provided that one be so divided between the two classes of criminals that they do not live or work in company. Such a separation is not only obviously necessary, but easy of accomplishment." Upon this I would remark that existing prisons can accommodate all first offenders, and that any new works should be made the exclusive home of incorrigibles.

WYMAN AND SONS, PRINTERS, GREAT QUEEN STREET, LONDON, W.C.

LINCOLN'S-INN
STEAM PRINTING & STATIONERY WORKS,
(NEAR THE INNS OF COURT AND THE BRITISH MUSEUM.)

WYMAN & SONS,
PRINTERS AND PUBLISHERS,

Undertake Every Description of

WOOD & COPPERPLATE ENGRAVING, LITHOGRAPHY, & BOOKBINDING.

TO AUTHORS AND OTHERS.—Messrs. WYMAN & SONS, PRINTERS, ENGRAVERS, STATIONERS, BOOKBINDERS, AND PUBLISHERS, invite the attention of Authors to the Facilities offered by their Establishment for the COMPLETE PRODUCTION of BOOKS of every description, all Departments of the Business being carried on under the immediate Personal Superintendence of the Firm. Inclusive Estimates promptly forwarded, and liberal arrangements made with Authors for the publication of their MSS., whether Scientific, Artistic, or Works of Fiction.

A MOST ELEGANT PRESENT FOR A LADY.

An Entirely Novel Work on Table Decoration. In Folio, with 24 Original Designs in Chromo-Lithography. Price Thirty Shillings.

Floral Designs for the Table:

Plain Directions for its Ornamentation with Cut Flowers and Fruit, Classified Lists of Suitable Plants, Leaves, Berries, &c.; and Twenty-four Original Coloured Designs for decorating Breakfast, Luncheon, Dinner, and Supper Tables at a moderate cost.

"We have no hesitation in saying that the work of Mr. Perkins now before us is one of the most elegant and useful gift-books of the present season. The very cover of it is a model of design and execution, and the whole get-up of the book does infinite credit to the Messrs. Wyman & Sons, who are the printers and publishers of it. Most, if not all, the designs are quite novel, and many of them are to be commended as much for their extreme simplicity as for their exquisite elegance."—*The Queen.*

"The production of this most beautiful and instructive volume is most opportune. It consists of a series of directions for the ornamentation of the table with leaves, flowers, and fruit, and it contains also classified lists of suitable plants, berries, and leaves for that purpose. Some of the designs are most beautiful ones, and the work, as a whole, is a most unconditional success. We can recommend any of our readers who are in want of a book on this subject to obtain one and judge for themselves. Many of the single designs are worth, to host or hostess, the money asked for the entire volume. The binding of the work is most handsome, forming in itself a table ornament."—*Land and Water.*

"This richly-ornamented volume comprises a series of original coloured designs, with directions for table decoration with leaves, flowers, and fruit; and, by the assistance of the letterpress, the reader will have no difficulty in perceiving the effect that is intended."—*Daily News.*

"The designs for the decoration of dinner, luncheon, and supper tables are, with scarcely an exception, perfect of their kind, and some few are absolutely perfect."—*Morning Advertiser.*

"Much taste and ingenuity have been displayed in the elaboration of the designs, and a fresh era in floral table decoration will be inaugurated by the present work."—*Court Journal.*

"The book contains a vast number of very pretty designs, and a list of the plants from which the decorations are to be selected."—*World.*

"The letterpress is illustrated by a series of illustrations, which, with their bright colour and artistic design, make the volume itself a work of art."—*Mayfair.*

74, 75, & 81, Great Queen Street, London, W.C.

Wyman & Sons, Printers, Publishers, &c.

Second Edition, 282 pages, demy 8vo. Profusely Illustrated, price 1s. 6d.

The Official Handbook of New Zealand.

A Collection of Papers by experienced Colonists, on the Colony as a whole, and on the several Provinces. Edited by Sir JULIUS VOGEL, K.C.M.G.

"This handbook is a work of considerable value and importance to all who are thinking of emigrating, and also to all who have commercial relations with our rising colony. It describes New Zealand from a New Zealand point of view, and has the advantages of being thoroughly reliable and authentic."—*Blackburn Standard.*

Second edition, demy 8vo., price 1s.; post-free, 1s. 1½d.

The England of the Pacific; or, New

Zealand as an English Middle-Class Emigration Field. By ARTHUR CLAYDEN, Author of "The Revolt of the Field," &c., who has just returned from a visit to the Colony.

There are Eight Full-page Illustrations, a Reprint of the Letters to the *Daily News* on the "English Agricultural Labourer in New Zealand," a Narrative of a Ride on Horseback through the North Island, Sketches of Settlers' Homes, and a variety of interesting particulars respecting New Zealand.

Crown 8vo., cloth gilt, price 12s.

Russia in 1870.

By HERBERT BARRY, late Director of the Chepeleffsky Estates and Iron Works in the Governments of Vladimir, Tambov, and Nijny Novgorod, Empire of Russia, Author of "Russian Metallurgical Works."

CONTENTS: On Mr. Dixon's Book "Free Russia;" Old Abuses and late Reforms; The People; Towns and Villages; Priests, Church, and Emperor; Sports and Pastimes; Manufactures and Trade; Ways and Communications; Siberia; The Great Fair of Nijny Novgorod; The Central Asian Question; Conclusion.

Price 1s. 6d.; post-free, 1s. 7d.; paper boards.

A Month in the Coasting Trade:

A True Narrative. By E. A., J. S. C., & J. A. R.

"This is a highly amusing account of a cruise in a vessel of small tonnage . . . . and worse sea stories have been written, and with more pretentiousness about them."—*Liverpool Mercury.*

"The work is very readable."—*Journal of Commerce.*

"We doubt not that a rapid sale of the work amongst the dwellers in inland towns will take place."—*Public Opinion.*

"This is an enjoyable book."—*Barrow Times.*

"Just the book for a seaside lounger."—*Daily Chronicle.*

"We congratulate the authors on the happy style in which the book is written, and recommend it."—*Bolton Chronicle.*

Price 1s., paper boards.

A £10 Tour.

By CAIRN LORGH. Descriptive of a Month's Holiday on the Continent for £10. Contains also Sketches of Excursions, of Fishing, and of Shooting Adventures.

In cloth gilt, price 3s.

The Mosquito Country.

A Holiday Tour in Norway, Lapland, and Sweden. By W. D. K.

74, 75, & 81, Great Queen Street, London, W.C.

Wyman & Sons, Printers, Publishers, &c.

Demy 8vo., cloth, price 10s. 6d.

Convict Life; or, Revelations concerning
CONVICTS AND CONVICT PRISONS. By a TICKET-OF-LEAVE MAN.

"If only half of the startling disclosures made by this intelligent convict be true, he has made out a strong case for Government interference."

Crown 8vo., cloth, price 6s.

The Felthams; or, Contrasts in Crime.
A story of thrilling interest, by FRANZ.

TO FREEMASONS.

Now ready, 1s. 6d., blue cloth; post free, 1s. 7d.

Masonic Points,
Being Authorized Cues in the Masonic Rituals of the E.A., F.C., and M.M. Degrees, and of those in the Royal Holy Arch. By Brother JADU.

Copy of Communication from H.R.H. the M.W.G.M.

"Freemasons' Hall, London, W.C.
25th October, 1876.

"DEAR SIR AND BROTHER,—I have this morning received a note from Mr. F. Knollys, Private Secretary to the Prince of Wales, requesting me to convey to you the thanks of his Royal Highness for the book you have been good enough to send him—a request with which I have much pleasure in complying.—I am, dear Sir, yours fraternally, JOHN HERVEY, G.S.

"To Bro. JADU, 74, Great Queen-street, W.C."

Demy 4to., price 6s.

Tables of Roman Law.
By M. A. FANTON, Docteur en Droit. Translated and edited by C. W. LAW, of the Middle Temple, Barrister-at-Law.

"Here, in fifteen Tables, we have the four books of the Institutes of Justinian, as to the ancient Roman law regarding persons, things, and actions. The first book gives some general notions respecting the meaning of the words *Justitia* and *Jus*, and treats of persons. The second, relating to things, treats of the means of acquiring particular objects, of successions to deceased persons, legacies, and trusts. The third deals with inheritances and obligations. The fourth treats of obligations and actions. The tables seem to be well translated and clearly arranged."—*The Builder.*

Third Edition, royal 8vo., cloth, price 5s.; post-free, 5s. 4d.

A Manual of the Statutes of Limitation.
Showing the time within which the ownership of property must be asserted and exercised, or actions commenced to prevent the operation of these statutes, viz.—Barring the remedy for obtaining or extinguishing the right to such property. By JAMES WALTER, Esq., Member of the Incorporated Law Society.

Second Edition, price 2s. 6d., cloth, flush.

A Manual of the Law of Mutual Life
ASSURANCE; to which are appended full Reports of the Decision of Lord Cairns in the Kent Mutual Society's Case, and of Mr. Justice Fry in Miss Winstone's Case in the Winding-up of the Albion Life Assurance Society. By THOMAS BRETT, LL.B.

74, 75, & 81, Great Queen Street, London, W.C.

Wyman & Sons, Printers, Publishers, &c.

WYMAN'S TECHNICAL SERIES.

In the Press.

Printing Machines and Machine Printing.

Being a Guide for Masters and Workmen. Containing Valuable Hints in the Selection of Machines—Practical Guide to Making Ready—Preparing Cuts—Cutting Overlays—Rollers—Useful Hints in Management of all kinds of Printing Machines—Details of the Construction of Machines, &c., &c., &c.

Crown 8vo., cloth, price 5s.; post-free, 5s. 4d.

The Grammar of Lithography.

A Complete and Practical Guide, for the Artist and Printer, in Commercial and Artistic Lithography, Chromo-Lithography, Zincography, Engraving on Stone, Photo-Lithography, and Lithographic Machine Printing, with an Appendix containing original Recipes for preparing Chalks, Inks, Transfer Papers, &c., &c. By W. D. RICHMOND.

The proof-sheets of this work have been revised by some of the most eminent men connected with the Art of Lithography, the result being a complete and reliable work.

Medium 4to., cloth gilt, bevelled boards, price 10s. 6d.

The Cabinet-Makers' Pattern Book.

First Series. Being Examples of Modern Furniture of the Character mostly in demand, selected from the Portfolios of the leading Wholesale Makers. To which are added Original Designs by First-rate Artists, comprising various Designs for Hall Furniture, Library Furniture, Dining-room Furniture, Drawing-room Furniture, and Bedroom Furniture.

"This will be found an invaluable work by the Master Cabinet-Maker and Upholsterer."

Crown 8vo., cloth, price 4s.; post-free, 4s. 4d.

The Practical Cabinet-Maker:

Being a Collection of Working Drawings of Furniture, with Explanatory Notes. By A WORKING MAN.

"No Master or Workman engaged in the Cabinet Trade should be without this useful Manual."

Second Edition, crown 8vo., cloth, price 2s.; post-free, 2s. 2d.

Workshop Management.

A Manual for Masters and Men, being practical remarks upon the Economic Conduct of Workshops, Trade Charities, &c. By FREDERIC SMITH.

"This book should be in the hands of every master and workman."

"The book is of none the less worth because the author happens to be modest. It is an acceptable contribution to industrial literature, being well penned, well ordered, and excellently presented by the publishers."—*Iron.*

Second Edition, crown 8vo., cloth, price 1s.; post-free, 1s. 1d.

English China and China Marks:

Being a Guide to the Principal Marks found on English Pottery and Porcelain. With Engravings of upwards of 150 Marks.

"The illustrations, which are very numerous, include marks from the fifteenth to the present century, and thus furnish a key to many of the puzzles with which collectors delight to concern themselves."—*City Press.*

74, 75, & 81, Great Queen Street, London, W.C.

Wyman & Sons, Printers, Publishers, &c.

Second Edition, price 6d. ; post-free, 7d.

A Key to one of the Main Difficulties of

ENGLISH ORTHOGRAPHY: Being an Alphabetical Collection of nearly 3,000 Words resembling others in Sound, yet differing in Sense, Spelling, or Accentuation. Compiled and arranged by HENRY BEADNELL.

Price 1s., cloth gilt, flush.

A Few Hints on Colour, and Printing in Colours. By P. B. WATT.

Monthly, price 1s. ; post-free, 1s. 2d.

The Theatre. (New Series).

A Monthly Review and Magazine. Each Number contains Photographic Portraits of a Distinguished Actress and Actor, and contains Theatrical Intelligence from all the chief Capitals of the World, with many Entertaining Anecdotes.

"The representative organ of the Theatrical Profession."—*Vide Press.*

The Theatre. (New Series.)

Volumes I. and II., handsomely bound, cloth gilt, price 8s. 6d. each.

These volumes contain each 12 exquisite cabinet size Photographic Portraits of the Celebrities of the Theatrical Profession, also contributions from the pens of the leading authors, together with many original articles, reviews and anecdotes, and the theatrical news of twelve months.

Price 1s. ; post-free, 1s. 1d.

The Desirability of Obtaining a National

THEATRE Not Wholly Controlled by the Prevailing Popular Taste. By GEORGE GODWIN, F.R.S., F.S.A.

Price 1s. ; post-free, 1s. 1d.

Suggestions for Establishing an English

ART THEATRE. By J. R. PLANCHÉ.

Paper cover, price 1s. ; post-free, 1s. 1d.

Montaser the Parricide:

An Eastern Drama in Five Acts. The Vision ; The Suicide ; Montaser in Hell ; Light ; The Slave of Death.

Crown 8vo., cloth, price 1s. 6d.

Æmilia.

A Drama of the Fourth Century, illustrating the Conflict between Paganism and Christianity.

74, 75, & 81, Great Queen Street, London, W.C.

Wyman & Sons, Printers, Publishers, &c.

Issued in Monthly Parts during the Session. Price 2s. 6d. to Non-Members.

Transactions of the Odontological Society of Great Britain.

Communications for the Editor of the " Transactions" to be addressed under cover to the Publishers,

Messrs. WYMAN & SONS, 74, 75, & 81, Great Queen Street, London, W.C.

Demy 8vo., cloth, price 1s. 6d.

The Condition of the Mouth and Teeth

DURING PREGNANCY. By OAKLEY COLES, Licentiate in Dental Surgery to the Royal College of Surgeons. Dental Surgeon to the Hospital for Diseases of the Throat.

8vo., cloth, price 2s. 6d.

Monarchy Defended :

A Treatise for Revolutionary Times. By JOHN VICKERS, Author of "The Slavery Quarrel," "Tinker Æsop," &c., &c.

Second Edition, cloth, price 2s. 6d.

Essays on the Dwellings of the Poor and OTHER SUBJECTS. By RUFUS USHER.

Fcap. 8vo., paper covers, price 1s. 6d.

An Invalid's Pastime :

Musings in an Infirmary Ward. By ARCHIBALD CAMERON. These effusions were composed to while away the tedious hours consequent on long confinement to a sick-room and sick-ward.

Price 1s., paper covers.

Burlingtonia.

Historical Notes about Burlington House, Piccadilly, and Neighbourhood.

" Burlington's beloved by every Muse."—*Gay's Trivia.*

Demy 8vo., paper covers, price 1s.

A Few Suggestions on Prayer - Book Reform. By GEORGE BILLER.

Price 1s.

Religion and Progress.

An Address by JOHN HENRY BRIDGES.

74, 75, & 81, Great Queen Street, London, W.C.

Wyman & Sons, Printers, Publishers, &c.,

Second Edition, crown 4to., price 1s.; post-free, 1s. 1d.

Wyman's Dictionary of Stationery and
COMPENDIUM OF USEFUL INFORMATION.
For the Office, Counting-house, and Library.

A CONTEMPORARY HISTORY OF THE WORLD.

Brief: the Week's News.

AN EPITOME OF THE PRESS FOR THE HOME CIRCLE, TRAVELLERS, AND RESIDENTS ABROAD.

Published in Weekly Numbers, price Twopence; and in Half-Yearly Volumes. Vol. I., cloth gilt, price 10s. Vols. II. and III., cloth gilt, 8s. each.

Volumes I. to III. embrace the period from November, 1878, *to July,* 1879.

These Volumes form a popular summary of the sayings and doings of the time, a short record of all noteworthy events, and a compendium of the manifold wit and wisdom of the entire press. A careful Index being published with each volume, they are most valuable as Works of Reference, and indispensable additions to all well-appointed libraries.

EVERYBODY'S WEEKLY PAPER.

Every Friday, price 2d. Ann. Sub. (in advance), 10s. 10d., post-free.

Brief: The Week's News.

An Epitome of the Press, for the Home Circle, Travellers, and Residents Abroad.

Brief: The Week's News is a Popular Summary of the Sayings and Doings of the Current Week; a short Record of Noteworthy Events; a Compendium of the manifold Wit and Wisdom of the entire Press; and a useful, handy Repertory of Facts, Dates, and Opinions, ready for future easy reference.

Brief: The Week's News aims to be a Journal alike for the busy and the idle; for him who has not time for much reading, and for him who has not inclination to read much; so that, without the labour of turning to one publication after another of the periodical Press, the reader of but slender leisure may, almost at a glance, keep himself abreast of all passing events, and fairly informed on all the questions of the day.

Brief: The Week's News is a necessary outcome of our very busy age. Brevity in speech and writing has become a necessity rather than a luxury. *Multum in parvo* is everywhere the order of the day. Condensation and compression meet us on all sides. And as in the material world, so in our literature. The hydraulic press is applied to the Press. Packing, not padding, is sought. It is the age of glances and glimpses; of terse phrases; of the news of the day "in a word;" of only half-hours with even the best authors; of French in four lessons, and all things in manuals. Letters have dwindled down to notes and memos, to postcards and telegrams.

Brief: The Week's News, presenting the Press compressed—concentrated essence of Press, in fact—giving a bird's-eye view of the contents of many Journals; marshalling together the different opinions of various Leaders of National Thought; impartially representing all Parties and Schools of Politics, Literature, Science, and Art, must appeal to a very large number of readers, and, while indispensable to many, prove acceptable to all.

Brief: The Week's News offers to the Advertiser at once a wide range and a long succession of the most eligible readers—not only in England, but also in the Colonies, India, and in all Countries where the English language is spoken.

74, 75, & 81, Great Queen Street, London, W.C.

Wyman & Sons, Printers, Publishers, &c.

With Illustrations of Furniture Designs and Working Drawings.
Every Saturday, price 4d. Yearly Subscription, including postage, 20s.; Half-yearly, 10s. payable in advance.

The Furniture Gazette.

AN ILLUSTRATED WEEKLY JOURNAL, TREATING OF ALL BRANCHES OF CABINET-WORK, UPHOLSTERY, AND INTERIOR DECORATION, BOTH AT HOME AND ABROAD.

INDISPENSABLE TO THE NUMEROUS TRADES CONCERNED.
Useful alike to the Connoisseur, the Antiquary, and the Householder.

The Publishers beg to call the attention of those who are not Subscribers to the *Furniture Gazette* to the strong claims of this Journal on the support of all who are interested in the Furniture, Upholstery, and Decoration Trades.

The *Furniture Gazette* has completed the Eleventh Volume of the New Series, and is the recognized organ of the important industries it represents—a fact shown not only by its continually increasing circulation, but by the steady demand for space both in its Literary and Advertising Departments.

Neither labour, care, nor expense is spared in the conduct of this Journal to secure matter of special practical value and interest to its Subscribers. Information carefully selected as to technical and artistic matters, as well as to the commercial, scientific, and mechanical branches of the numerous Trades within the province of the *Furniture Gazette*, may always be found in its pages. Amongst the subjects thus generally treated of and watchfully recorded in its columns, the following may be indicated :—

- The various Manufactures appertaining to Furniture, Upholstery, and Decoration, in all their numerous branches of Wood, Metal, Porcelain, Woven Fabrics, Paper, &c., with the Materials, Tools, and Appliances peculiar to each.
- Working Drawings from Practical Authorities.
- The state of Home and Foreign Markets, with a special view to Imports and Exports, and the fluctuations of Supply and Demand.
- Suggestions for Useful and Attractive Novelties in Materials and Manufactures.
- Recent Patents and Improvements.
- Scientific Principles, Inventions, and Discoveries affecting Manufactures, Materials, or Machinery.
- Decorative Works in progress or newly completed, with careful and accurate Descriptions, illustrated, where necessary, with Wood Engravings.
- Changes in Fashion, Actual and Prospective.
- Ecclesiastical Furniture and Decoration.
- Art Exhibitions, Art Schools, and Reports of Lectures on Art in connection with Furniture and Upholstery Manufactures.
- Current Prices, Trade Reports, Tables of Exports, and minor Trade Jottings.
- Legal and Police Intelligence affecting the represented Trades. News, Notes, and Comments. Useful Hints. "Short Ends Corner" for Workmen. Practical Papers by Practical Workmen, &c. Correspondence. Answers to Correspondents, &c.

Weekly, price 6d. Annual Subscription, £1. 1s.; with Monthly Marine Supplement, £1. 5s.

The Review.

A First-class Paper on all matters connected with Fire, Life, and Marine Insurance.

Published on the 15th of each Month. Price 6d. Annual Subscription (payable in advance), 7s. 6d. post-free.

The Printing Times and Lithographer:

A Technical and Fine-Art Journal, devoted to Typography, Lithography, and the Reproductive Arts.

The *Printing Times and Lithographer* is a medium of communication between all who are associated with the Art of Printing in its manifold forms. Having no separate interests to serve, it is not the organ of any one class or trade, but deals with every topic impartially and fearlessly. It has gained a high reputation for the great value and interest of its contents. Writers of experience and special knowledge are its contributors;

74, 75, & 81, Great Queen Street, London, W.C.

Wyman & Sons, Printers, Publishers, &c.

while gentlemen well known in the Scientific and Art World co-operate with the conductors to render the Journal a complete and authoritative exponent of the current progress of the Graphic Arts.

All new Works of interest to the Printing Profession receive an early and impartial criticism. Especial attention continues to be paid to the new modes of Automatic Engraving which are constantly being introduced in Great Britain and Abroad ; and illustrations of their capabilities, with details of their practical working, are given.

Amongst the many subjects treated of are the Press, as it is affected by the restrictions placed upon it from time to time by Government Departments, &c. ; the Law of Copyright as it affects Newspaper Proprietors, Authors, Publishers, Type-Founders, &c. ; the advances made in the Art of Printing ; the production of New Publications ; an account of all New Inventions ; a chronicle of Passing Events ; the management and progress of the various Trade Charities ; the operations of Workmen's Unions and Combinations among Manufacturers, &c. Its pages are open to the free discussion of all questions upon which its readers may desire to interchange opinions by way of Correspondence. The *Printing Times and Lithographer* derives its information from, and circulates in all parts of the World ; and no pains are spared to ensure the accuracy of its intelligence, and to render it in every respect worthy the support of Lithographers, Letterpress Printers, Artists, Antiquaries, and Literary Men generally.

Being a thoroughly-established Journal—one which is both carefully read and preserved—and possessing a large and increasing circulation at Home and Abroad, the *Printing Times and Lithographer* presents an exceptionally good medium for the publication of the Announcements and Advertisements of Type Founders, Printers' Engineers, Inventors, Manufacturers, and of all who are associated with the Art of Printing in its various branches.

FOURTH YEAR OF PUBLICATION.
Crown 4to., price 2s. 6d., stiff boards.

The Furniture Gazette Diary and Desk-book for 1880.

A complete and useful Office Diary and Desk-book, interleaved with blotting-paper, adapted to the requirements of the Cabinet, Upholstery, and Decorative Trades throughout the Country. The Diary contains, in addition to the usual business information, a carefully-compiled and authentic Directory of the Trades allied to Furnishing, reprinted from *The Furniture Gazette.*

SECOND YEAR OF PUBLICATION.
Crown 4to., price 2s. 6d., stiff boards.

The Printing Trades' Diary and Desk-book for 1880.

The Printing Trades' Diary and Desk-book for 1880 is compiled with a view to meeting the everyday requirements of Principals, Overseers, and Managers, connected with the Letterpress Printing, Lithographic, Stationery, Bookbinding, and Auxiliary Trades. In addition to the usual General, Commercial, and Legal Information, it will contain :— A Diary, three days on a page, interleaved with Blotting-Paper ; the London Compositors' Scales of Prices for News and Bookwork, Revised and Annotated ; Abstracts of the Scottish and Provincial Scales of Prices ; an Epitome of the Law of Libel and Copyright, as affecting Printers and Newspaper Proprietors ; Tables for the Printers' Warehouse, relating to the Sizes and giving out of Paper, Cardboard, &c. ; Tables for the Storeroom, the Economy of Types, Materials, &c. ; Various Useful Forms, Recipes, Memoranda, &c. &c. Merely elementary information is avoided, as the aim of the compilers is to present, in a convenient and accessible form, only useful matter, which, in the course of his ordinary occupation, the master tradesman may at any time require. All the Reference Tables have been carefully compiled, and the Recipes actually tested.

74, 75, & 81, Great Queen Street, London, W.C.

Wyman & Sons, Printers, Publishers, &c.

In cloth gilt, price 5s.

The Review Almanack for 1880.

CONTENTS:—Calendar of Principal Events for 1880; Astronomical Notes of the Month; Register of Events; Almanack for 200 Years; Table of English and Scottish Sovereigns; the Royal Family of England; the House of Lords; Irish and Scotch Peers (not being Peers of Parliament); the House of Commons; the Ministry; List of Judges and Magistrates; H.M. Privy Council; List of Archbishops and Bishops; British and Foreign Ambassadors; Corporation of the City of London; London School Board; Metropolitan Board of Works; Banks and Bankers in London; List of Country Bankers; Institutions and Societies; Lords-Lieutenant in England and Wales; Metropolitan Fire Brigade Stations; Marine Insurance Brokers' Guide; Life Assurance Premiums; Directory of Insurance Companies Transacting Business in the United Kingdom; Directors of Insurance Companies; Lists of Managers, Secretaries, and the other Officers of Insurance Companies; List of the Principal Insurance Agents in Great Britain; List of Members of the Society of Actuaries, the Actuaries' Club, and of the Faculty of Actuaries in Scotland; Life Insurance Companies' Accounts for the last Nine years; Fire and Marine Companies in the United States; Life Insurance Companies in the United States.

THIRTEENTH YEAR OF PUBLICATION.
PRICE SIXPENCE. PUBLISHED IN OCTOBER OF EACH YEAR.
In an Illuminated Wrapper, beautifully printed in Old-Style Type, on Toned Paper.

Everybody's Year-book for 1880.

A Useful and Popular Annual, containing Something for Everybody all the Year Round.

The Cheapest and Best Gift-book of the Day.

CONTENTS:

Fixed and Movable Festivals; Holidays at the Public Offices; Date of Creation of some Festivals; Jewish Calendar; Mahometan Calendar; Law Sittings; Law Terms; University Terms; Eclipses; Transfer and Dividend Days; An Almanack and Calendar of the Events of the Year; Story of the Months; Age of the Moon; Rising and Setting of the Sun; Time of High Water at London Bridge; Phases of the Moon; Things to be borne in Mind; Astronomical Notes of the Month; Table of High Water at nearly 200 of the principal Ports; A Perpetual Almanack for finding the Day of the Month; Table for Calculating Interest; Family Ready-Reckoner; Interest Table; Tables of the Sovereigns of England and Scotland; The Royal Family; Sovereigns of Europe; The National Debt; Archbishops and Bishops of the Established Church; Supreme Court of Judicature; Her Majesty's Ministers and Chief Officers of State; Her Majesty's Household; H.R.H. The Prince of Wales's Household; Her Majesty's Privy Council; Lords Lieutenant of Counties in the United Kingdom; Officers of the Houses of Parliament; British and Foreign Ambassadors; Consulate Offices in London; Metropolitan County Courts; Assessed Taxes; Stamp Duties; Corporation of the City of London; School Board for London; Metropolitan Board of Works; Bank of England; London Banks; Cab Regulations; Postal Information; English Weights and Measures; How to make your Will; Distribution of Intestate Estates; Languages and Alphabets; Prevailing Winds; Money and Coinage; Foreign Moneys and their English Equivalents; French Weights and Measures; The Sportsman's Calendar; Multum-in-Parvo Guide to the Principal Places of Amusement and Chief Points of Interest in London and its Suburbs; List of the Principal London Restaurants; List of Seaside Resorts; Mode of Addressing Persons of Rank; The Ball-Room Guide; and a large amount of Information Useful to Everybody All the Year Round.

"We notice that the editions for 1868 and 1869 have been reprinted, and, having made frequent reference to them ourselves, we can with confidence recommend them as being very useful. All who desire a really good year-book should purchase the 'Everybody's.'"—*Rugby Gazette.*

"It has been carefully compiled, is nicely printed on toned paper, has an attractive cover, and should find its way into every house and place of business in the kingdom. Those wishing to invest sixpence in a book will find this the very thing for them."—*Banbury Guardian.*

"'Everybody's Year-book' has a much better claim to the title than a good many publications and things which appeal to 'everybody.'"—*City Press.*

"We may congratulate Messrs. Wyman & Sons on the excellent and varied character of the work, and for its typographical merit."—*Salford Chronicle.*

"This very popular annual is of the practical and useful rather than the merely ornamental kind, and contains a good deal of solid information necessary to the family and household. The work is altogether a valuable addition to the family library."—*Rochdale Observer.*

*** *Owing to the constant demand for complete sets, the Publishers will be happy to exchange the current issue of Everybody's Year-book for copies of Everybody's Year-book for 1874.*

74, 75, & 81, Great Queen Street, London, W.C.

www.ingramcontent.com/pod-product-compliance
Lightning Source LLC
Chambersburg PA
CBHW032133230426
43672CB00011B/2325